SANDI GENOVESE'S
Three~Dimensional Scrapbooks

Techniques for
building texture
& style into
your pages

QUARRY

First published in the United States of America
by Quarry Books, an imprint of
Rockport Publishers, Inc.
33 Commercial Street
Gloucester, Massachusetts 01930-5089
Telephone: (978) 282-9590
Fax: (978) 283-2742
www.rockpub.com

Library of Congress Cataloging-in-Publication Data
Genovese, Sandi.
    Sandi Genovese's three-dimensional scrapbooks:
techniques for building texture and style into
your pages/ Sandi Genovese.

        p.   cm.

    ISBN 1-56496-997-5 (pbk.)
    1. Photograph albums. 2. Scrapbooks.
3. Assemblage (Art) I. Title.

TR465.G473 2003

    745.593—dc21   2003009397
                                                    CIP

ISBN: 1-56496-997-5

10 9 8 7 6 5 4 3

COVER DESIGN: Laura McFadden Design, Inc.
laura.mcfadden@rcn.com

COVER IMAGE: Bobbie Bush Photography
www.bobbiebush.com

PHOTOGRAPHY: Bobbie Bush Photography
www.bobbiebush.com

PROJECT MANAGER
AND COPYEDITOR: Lindsay Stoms

PROOFREADER: Krista Fuller

Printed in China

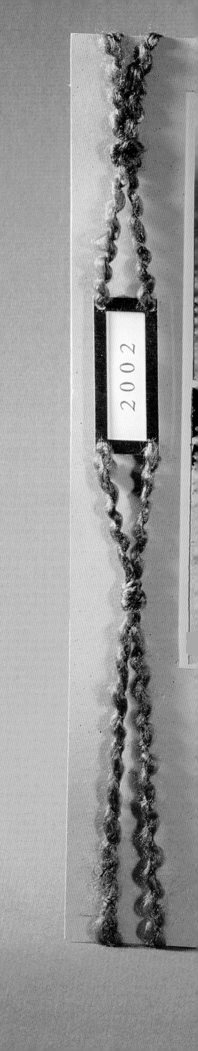

One of Landon's Easter eggs from Grandma and Grandpa promised him a trip to the zoo, so Memorial Day weekend we decided to call them on it. We all made the 3 hour drive to the closest zoo in St. Louis. The kids really enjoyed seeing all of the animals and our family had a great time together.

Contents

Rosemary Ann Wilson - 1947

Introduction

The advent of 3-D scrapbook pages has added another dimension to the scrapbooking world—literally! Everyday materials that you find at hardware, office supply, and fabric stores are appearing on scrapbook store shelves, repackaged and sometimes made archivally safe. It's been an incredibly exciting discovery, leaving one to wonder, "What will scrapbookers be adding to their pages next?"

Within this book you will discover some awe-inspiring textured designs that will make you want to reach out and fondle the pages (which, unfortunately, are flat). You will see how adding materials such as layered papers, die-cuts, beads, glass, metals, fabrics, ribbons, keepsakes, and natural objects can give a scrapbook page depth and sparkle. Dimensional elements, such as a seashell, can evoke a magical memory and create a tangible link to a cherished point in time.

If you are concerned that adding 3-D elements will clutter your pages, don't dismay. If a clean, pared-down look is more your style, you can still achieve dimensionality with only one or two elements. Sometimes a single textural object can serve as a powerful focal point. This book contains a wide array of styles—some that successfully incorporate several 3-D items and others that keep it simple with just a few embellishment pops.

I've tried to anticipate your questions and provide all the tips and techniques, materials, and style information that a scrapper could want. And, since most crafty scrappers have found uses for their supplies beyond scrapbooking, each chapter in this book contains a project that moves off the scrapbook page and into other photo-based projects. For those who practice "flat" scrapbooking, the addition of metals, glass, and fabrics might seem dangerous to the preservation of photos. Happily, manufacturers have taken care to make many of these materials photo-friendly, and I've included an abundance of information in this book to help you protect your photos and preserve your albums for years to come.

Working on this book has provided me with a newfound appreciation for the amazing talent that exists within our craft. As much as I enjoyed the creative process of designing my own projects, I was awed and inspired by the projects created by my friends, and I thank them for sharing. I'm sure you will be as dazzled as I am by the array of styles and artistry in this book. Enjoy!

—Sandi Genovese

1

Basics

If you are diving into 3-D scrapbooking, you have probably been introduced to the basics of this craft and have a few pages under your belt and a cache of supplies in your closet. When designing with 3-D embellishments, I find myself frequently using tweezers for picking up and placing small objects, mini craft scissors for snipping ribbon and cutting fine detail, a personal die-cutting system for creating die-cut shapes and titles, and wire cutters for snipping and bending wire. A hammer, eyelet punch, and eyelet setter are necessary for, of course, setting eyelets and fastening all the other metal embellishments that require the setter. And a ruler, craft knife, and self-healing mat are general essentials for precision cutting.

Adhesives will be an important consideration. There are many different kinds of acid-free adhesives on the market, but you need to decide which one will work best depending on the embellishment you are using. Some items that have a shiny metallic surface or a bumpy texture will require a more aggressive adhesive than others. Glue dots, foam adhesive, and scrappy tape are all aggressive adhesives. Less aggressive, but highly dependable, are adhesive machines, such as Xyron, and acid-free double-sided tape.

Perhaps the most important factor to consider when creating 3-D pages is safety. One of the reasons we scrapbook is to preserve photos for generations to come. As we start adding textural items to our pages, it becomes even more important to maintain a protective, acid-free environment. There are a number of ways to achieve this in the realm of dimensionality.

Keep it acid-free

When adding 3-D paper-based items to your layouts that you aren't sure are acid-free, there are a few things you can do to insure protection for your albums and memorabilia. If you incorporate items such as road maps, menus, or newspaper clippings on your page, follow these three simple rules:

- **Test it.** Use a pH testing pen to test the level of acidity in the item.
- **Spray it.** There are now sprays on the market that neutralize the acid in paper-based materials. Simply spray the entire paper item, and it will be preserved and protected.
- **Copy it.** If you are really unsure about the item, one of the easiest solutions is to make a color photocopy of it onto acid-free paper.

There are a variety of 3-D embellishments and stickers available in scrapbook stores, many of which are produced for scrapbook pages and are acid-free.

Safe design

When designing your layout, a little careful planning can make all the difference between album preservation and disintegration. Make sure that 3-D objects that aren't labeled "acid-free" don't come in contact with your photos—and that includes the photos on the facing page. When you close your album, you don't want 3-D objects pressing into the photos on the opposite page leaving scratches, tears, or imprints. Plastic page protectors will also prevent damage, though

the glare will diminish the texture and dimensionality of a 3-D page.

Also, pay attention to the placement of 3-D objects throughout the album. If you like adding enhancements to your page titles, which are often at the top of the page, you will likely be left with a giant bulge along the top of your album when you close it. Over time, that will warp and disfigure your entire album. Vary the placement of your embellishments throughout the album—it's not only good for the health of the album, but it's good for your creative health, too.

Safe storage

The best way to store your albums, even if you aren't using textured items, is to place them upright on a shelf. Laying them flat puts pressure on the pages, and, if you are using 3-D embellishments, it could lead to damaging impressions.

Refer to the tips and instructions for each project for additional insights on tools and creating safe pages. You'll be amazed at the wealth of ideas you'll find in these pages and will no doubt start looking at everyday objects with a newfound appreciation for their creative possibilities.

2

Paper

LAYERING PAPERS, DIE-CUTS, POP-UPS, AND FOLDOUTS

The incredible variety and versatility of paper is enough to make your head spin. Walk into any scrapbook or craft store and you will be faced with racks of dazzling colors, designs, and textures. But while you might think of paper as flat, there are a number of techniques you can use to manipulate paper into dimensional designs.

In this chapter, you will learn how to add depth and texture to your pages with paper, card stock, and vellum. Paper engineering can be as simple as raising designs with pop-dots or as intricate as multiple layered pop-ups. Using paper die-cuts is a quick and inexpensive way to add character to your pages. Whether you have a personal die-cutting system at home, use the machine at your local scrapbook store, or buy pre-made die-cuts, look for shapes that include perforation marks that denote detail. Those perforation marks serve as guides to help you layer paper onto the die-cut to create beautiful, nuanced designs.

Pop-ups and sliders might sound like baseball terms, but in the scrapbook world they serve as interactive paper ele-

ments that add motion and surprise. Paper mosaics create a ceramic tile effect from cutting and reassembling small pieces of paper. Vellum windows offer a sneak peak of the photo or journaling underneath. Folding, creasing, embossing, cutting, punching, quilling, tearing, layering—whew! What a workout! But all those active terms will bring visual interest and liveliness to your pages.

As you shop for paper, the most important things to look for are the words "acid-free" and "lignin-free." The heart of scrapbooking lies in long-term preservation—capturing memories to share with your family and future generations. If your paper isn't labeled "acid-free," it's wise to check the pH-level of your paper in order to protect your photos and maintain the artistry of your books. Thick, handmade papers add warmth and texture, but make sure they are archivally safe. Shop for paper at scrapbook, craft, rubber stamp, stationery, and art stores, or on the Internet. And let the paper games begin!

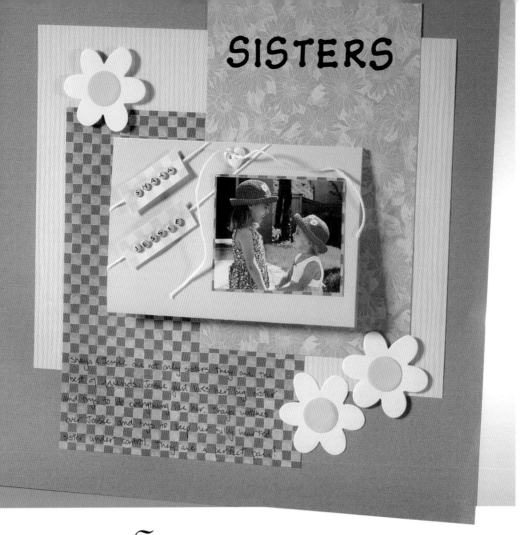

Sisters

Brads and buttons are a fast and easy way to add embellishments. They come in a variety of colors, shapes, and sizes.

MATERIALS

plain paper

patterned paper

embroidery floss

press-on letters

brads

buttons

adhesive

foam adhesive

scissors

die-cutting machine and dies

1. Start with a 12" x 12" (30.5 cm x 30.5 cm) blue background page. Arrange and layer three coordinating patterned papers onto the background page.

2. Accordion fold yellow paper into three separate panels and attach to the center of the page.

3. Mat photographs in a complementary patterned paper. Place a photo on each panel, making sure the photograph on the cover is slightly smaller.

4. Cut two small rectangles out of yellow patterned paper. Spell out each person's name using white brads and rub-on letters. Attach the finished brads to the yellow rectangles.

5. Place a white piece of embroidery floss behind each finished rectangle and attach the finished rectangles to the accordion card. Secure the excess thread with tape on the back of the card.

6. Attach a white heart button at the top of the card with embroidery floss. Leave the thread long to use as a pull to open the accordion card.

7. Die-cut the daisies out of white and yellow paper. On the yellow daisies, cut around the perforation marks in the center. Place the yellow circles onto the white daisies. Arrange the finished daisies onto the page using foam adhesive to create dimension.

8. Add press-on letters at the top to create a title and a journaling block at the bottom to tell the story.

Hunting for chestnuts

Layering with paper is a simple yet effective way
to add dimension to scrapbook pages.

1. Cut a narrow rectangular frame out of paper that matches the background paper. The frame should be slightly smaller than the photo it will encase.

2. Run leaf-patterned paper through an adhesive machine to apply adhesive before cutting out the individual leaves.

3. Fasten the leaves to the frame, occasionally raising leaves with foam adhesive.

4. Crop and mat additional photos and a title bar.

5. Die-cut leaves from fall-colored papers and fasten them to the page where journaling will be placed.

6. Tear a piece of vellum, journal in a black pen, and attach over the die-cut leaves with a nail head in each corner.

MATERIALS

plain paper

patterned paper

vellum

leaf die-cuts

nail heads

foam adhesive

scissors

black pen

adhesive machine, such as a Xyron

DESIGNER: SANDI GENOVESE

What a card!

Add additional dimension to stamped images by raising them off the page with foam adhesive.

1. Stamp stars and hearts onto card stock in contrasting colors and cut out the images.

2. Stamp vertical stripes along the bottom quarter of the background page using a watermark ink pad. Visually separate the bottom quarter of the page from the top three quarters by placing a horizontal strip of grosgrain ribbon along the top edge of the vertical stripes.

3. Add additional embellishments, such as buttons and embroidery floss, to the stamped images.

4. Place the hearts and stars on the page in a repeating pattern.

5. Stamp the title. Repeat the star and heart on the header.

The tree

String fiber across a photograph to recreate the look of a wrapped package as well as add some dimension to the page.

1. Place a strip of corrugated paper across the top of the layout. Cut the title out of card stock and glue to the corrugated strip.

2. Tear a strip of contrasting colored card stock and adhere it to the center third of the background page.

3. String fiber across one of the photos. Place both photos onto the background paper.

4. Type journaling on vellum, tear the top and bottom, adhere to the page, and place fiber along the left and right edges of the vellum.

5. Using a paper punch, cut three pinecones from card stock, double-mat them onto three rectangles, and place them side-by-side to tie the theme together.

MATERIALS

card stock

corrugated paper

fiber

scissors

paper punch

personal computer

Peace

Layer vellum, sheer black ribbon, and matted, stamped squares of card stock in varying shades of black and silver. The simplicity of light and dark colors creates visual interest that is stunning.

DESIGNER: KELLY JONES

MATERIALS

card stock

vellum

ribbon

foam adhesive

rubber stamp

ink pad

scissors

gel pen

1. Double-mat the photograph with a small black border and a larger white one, and then place the photograph onto black card stock to make the picture stand out.

2. Across the bottom, layer a piece of vellum on the card stock, sheer ribbon over the vellum, and then adhere three evenly-spaced squares onto the ribbon, raising them with foam adhesive.

3. Cut black card stock into 2" (5 cm) squares and stamp a pattern that relates to the photograph. Adhere 2" (5 cm) squares to larger squares, using foam adhesive to raise them.

4. Write the page title with a gel pen.

DESIGNER: JENNA BEEGLE

Rosemary Ann Wilson

Paper can be pleated in the same way as fabric for a terrific three-dimensional effect.

1. Cut approximately eight strips of patterned paper 12" long x 1" wide (30.5 cm x 2.5 cm).

2. Using an embossing or scoring tool, score lines along the green paper, measuring ¼" (6 mm), then ¾" (1.9 cm), then ¼" (6 mm), then ¾" (1.9 cm), continuing until the end of the paper is reached. This will create lines for folding the pleats. Using this pleat, a 12" (30.5 cm) strip of paper will be 6" (15.2 cm) long when pleated.

3. Mount the pleats along the sides of a sheet of ivory card stock and miter the corners.

4. Trim a second sheet of patterned paper in a coordinating print to 11" (27.9 cm).

MATERIALS

patterned paper

card stock

vellum

journaling block

wire-stemmed paper flowers

foam adhesive

glue dots

scissors

embossing or scoring tool

paper trimmer

Mat with another coordinating patterned paper, leaving approximately ⅛"
(3 mm) around the floral.

5. Mat the photo with ivory card stock and pink patterned paper.

6. Adhere a larger vellum mat to the floral page, then mount the photo onto that
   using foam adhesive.

7. Roughly lay out the position of the flowers around the photo and connect them
   by twisting the bottom of the wire stem around the next flower's stem. This will
   lock them together. Doing this with the flowers in place will help to achieve
   perfect placement. Adjust the leaves and flowers as desired and glue the
   flowers into place with mini glue dots.

8. Handwrite the child's name and date in a pre-cut journaling block to complete
   the page.

Patchwork garden quilt

Use card stock and stickers to fashion a purse that is three-dimensional
and can be used to hold a removeable journaling card.

MATERIALS

plain paper

patterned paper

vellum

ribbon

stickers

gift card

foam adhesive

baby powder

scissors

glue or tape

1. Cut photographs and accent paper into nine equal-sized squares.
   Trim the accent paper with sliver stickers and place grass stickers
   along the bottom edge of four of the accent paper squares.

2. Place the various puppy stickers onto the squares. Use foam
   adhesive to pop a second puppy on top of the first one in the
   top two squares. Cut segments of grass and pop them over
   the top of the existing grass for greater dimension. The same
   technique can be done with the daffodils in the right square
   by placing daffodils (with their stems cut off) over the top
   of the existing flowers.

3. Pop the baby carriage in the lower left square so that the puppy appears to be
   inside the carriage. To create the square with the gate, carefully place a second
   gate on the back of the first one. Place the bottles at the top and bottom of the
   gate to create hinges. Use baby powder to neutralize the glue on the segment
   of bottles that hang over the edge of the gate. Fold the bottles around the edge
   of the gate, trimming them slightly.

4. Cut small squares of foam adhesive and attach them to the fold under the
   baby bottles.

5. After attaching the gate to the square with the foam adhesive, place the shrubs
   and trees, popping them so that the right side of the gate can rest on them
   when it is closed.

6. Each 3-D butterfly requires three stickers. Begin with either a blue or yellow
   butterfly, and alternate the colors. Attach the right wing of the first butterfly to
   the left wing of the second butterfly, and then attach the right wing of the second

butterfly to the left wing of the third butterfly. Attach the 3-D butterfly to the page with the remaining two "unstuck" wings. This will become easier with practice!

7. Attach the squares to the page, alternating them with four photographs of the same size. Place the blank accent paper square in the center after attaching a 4" x 2¼" (10.2 cm x 5.7 cm) vellum pocket to it. Create the pocket by folding in the sides of the vellum ½" (1.3 cm) each and the bottom ¼" (.6 cm) and sliding the gingham square into the pocket.

8. Complete the page by creating the journaling purse. Using a small yellow gift card (or yellow card stock), cut the edges so that they taper in at the top of the card, where the fold is. Attach the ribbon handle with tape or glue, and trim the edges of the purse with stickers. Top it off with a popped dog bone.

9. Trim the inside of the purse with sliver stickers, a butterfly, and a brush and comb to complete the page.

DESIGNER: BARB WENDEL/KELLY CAROLLA

How long is a girl a child?

Paper quilling is a simple technique that adds dimension and elegance to a scrapbook page.

MATERIALS

patterned paper

card stock

printed frame

adhesive

quilling tool

scalloped scissors

craft knife

BASIC QUILLING SHAPES

- Tight circle/ peg
- Loose circle/ closed coil
- Teardrop
- Marquise/eye
- Shaped marquise/leaf
- Square
- Heart/rolled heart/shield
- Loose coil scroll
- Scroll heart
- V scroll
- C scroll
- S scroll

1. Cut along one edge of cream card stock with scalloped scissors. From each scallop, make downward slits in the card stock almost to the bottom edge. Roll these pieces with the quilling tool to make the flowers, spreading petals when finished.

2. From cream card stock strips, create eleven marquise-shaped leaves and sixteen tight circles. (Refer to the Basic Quilling Shapes diagram.) Attach a strip of cream card stock to the black card stock as a stem, curving up the page. Attach flowers, leaves, and dots.

3. Mount a strip of black card stock to the left side of the patterned paper background. Cut strips from second patterned paper and apply them to the background.

4. Mount a photo in the frame and mount on the page. Mount a journaling block onto the other piece of black card stock, adding quilled details as desired.

DESIGNER: JENNA BEEGLE

How long is a girl a child?
Sarah - 5 Years Old

Jenna Carol Johnston - 14 Months

Jenna Carol Johnston

Create a unique border with paper quilled flowers, leaves, and vines.

MATERIALS

patterned paper

card stock

journaling block

ribbon photo corners

adhesive

scissors

1. Begin with a 12" x 12" (30.5 cm x 30.5 cm) page of blue gingham paper.

2. Cut a smaller square of patterned paper to sit in the middle of the blue gingham page. Mat that with ivory card stock and attach it to the page.

3. Use blue card stock strips to create thirty-two leaf-shaped pieces for flower petals and thirty-six smaller leaf-shaped pieces for leaves. (Refer to the Basic Quilling Shapes diagram on page 20.) Use cream card stock to create ivory flower centers and mount them on each corner of the page. Add petals to the flowers. Add strips of cream card stock as stems between the flowers; add leaves.

4. Mount a photo using ribbon corners and a small journaling block.

DESIGNER: ANDREA GROSSMAN

Antarctica page

Incorporate multiple photos onto one page with a unique accordion folding technique.

MATERIALS

plain paper

vellum

stickers

black tape

scissors

craft knife

journaling pen

pencil

1. Border one sheet of black cover paper with silver sliver stickers and miter the corners.

2. Using a sheet of lined paper underneath, handwrite journaling onto vellum and, using transparent photo squares, affix a journaling panel to the background paper with an even border all around.

3. To make the foldout, cut four rectangles 4 ¼" x 6 ¼" (10.8 cm x 15.9 cm) from the additional black papers and tape them together from the back, leaving a sliver of space between so they will fold up. Attach photos.

4. For the cover panel, cut another rectangle of black paper 6 ¼" x 4 ¾" (15.9 cm x 12.1 cm). Score it ½" (1.3 cm) from the top.

5. From the back, tape the top of the first photo panel and foldout to the bottom edge of the cover panel.

6. Position your foldout on the page, then mark with a pencil at each top corner of the foldout. With a craft knife, cut a line from dot to dot. Slip the top of the foldout through the slit and tape it to the back of the page.

7. Using identical snowflake stickers, stick one on the front bottom edge photo panel in the foldout and one back-to-back on the back of that panel.

8. Mount the journaling panel under the foldout.

Domo Arigato

Add a touch of ancient times to your page by creating a scroll with paper that has been distressed with water.

1. Stamp the left half of the background paper. Mat onto a slightly larger piece of complementary colored paper.

2. Stamp the title onto a contrasting colored paper. Mat the title onto the background paper and adhere to the page.

3. Journal onto white card stock. Tear the long edges and stamp the fan border with mustard ink over the journaling, stamping off once first to lighten the image.

4. Spray the journaling piece with water and distress the paper. Roll the top and bottom to form a scroll and allow to dry.

5. Trim black pieces to fit behind the fans and the journaling.

6. Crimp the pieces and mount the fans and journaling as shown.

7. Mount the photos onto card stock and adhere to the background page as shown.

MATERIALS

card stock

adhesive

rubber stamps

ink pads, watermark

water bottle and water

scissors

journaling marker

paper crimper

DESIGNER: SHELLI GARDNER

MATERIALS

plain paper
patterned paper
card stock
foam adhesive
scissors
stylus
plastic spoon
pigment marker
die-cutting machine
alphabet and
wave dies

1st dive

Layering die-cuts with foam adhesive adds dimension. Take it one step further and give some shape to the die-cut with paper tolling.

1. Cut various-sized waves from complementary blue papers.

2. To paper tole: Turn a wave to the back side. Using the back of a plastic spoon, rub from the center out across the entire surface. The paper will begin to curl. Then trace the outline of the paper shape with a stylus. Repeat this for each wave.

3. Layer and arrange the waves with foam adhesive.

4. For the title, die-cut letters and numbers. Use foam adhesive to lift alternate letters. Outline some letters with a pigment marker to make letters stand out against the background.

5. Silhouette and mat photos, and then adhere. Journal as desired.

Analisa

Create multidimensional scrapbook pages with foam adhesive that help images or elements pop out from the background.

1. Cut a strip of turquoise paper and place it across the top of a red 12" x 12" (30.5 cm x 30.5 cm) scrapbook page.

2. Using a paper trimmer, cut ½" (1.3 cm) strips of gold and yellow paper. Arrange the strips on the page, alternating each color. Vary the height of each strip by adding foam adhesive.

3. Cut a photograph into ½" (1.3 cm) strips like the gold and yellow paper. Place a strip of picture onto each yellow piece of paper.

4. Hang an eyelet letter from the strips of yellow paper to spell out a name. Attach the letters with thread and heart stickers.

5. Die-cut the teeth out of white and cream paper. Cut away detail and layer to create shading.

6. Double-mat a journaling rectangle and place it on the page at a diagonal. Attach the finished teeth to the corner of the rectangle.

MATERIALS

plain paper

embroidery floss

stickers

adhesive

foam adhesive

eyelet setting tool and eyelet letters

pre-cut die-cuts or die-cutting machine and dies

paper trimmer

MATERIALS

plain paper

zebra paper

ribbon

stickers

silver charm

adhesive

foam adhesive

silver pen

eyelet word

eyelet setting tool

pre-cut die-cuts
or die-cutting
machine and dies

Tag along mini memory book

The accordion pleats in this mini book create a wonderful dimensionality even before the addition of ribbon and metal charms. When the album is closed, all the tags sit up; but as the album is opened, the tags form a crisscrossing pattern.

1. Cut a red strip of paper 6" x 17" (15.2 cm x 43.2 cm).

2. Accordion fold the middle section into four evenly spaced pleats, allowing 6" (15.2 cm) on each end for the front and back covers.

3. Line the inside front and back cover with zebra paper (allow a slight edge of red to show all around). Mat a photo and a journaling panel and center them inside each front and back inside cover.

4. Die-cut twelve black tags and thread a red ribbon through each tag hole.

5. Attach the first four tags onto the front side of each pleat. Attach the middle row of tags onto the back side of each pleat. Attach the final four tags onto the front side of each pleat. There should be a slight gap between each row of tags allowing the tags to form a crisscrossing pattern when the album is opened.

6. Decorate each tag with photos, die-cuts, stickers, and journaling (with a silver pen). Three-dimensional embellishments, such as a silver heart charm, can be added where desired.

7. Mat the title of the album and attach it to the front cover.

8. Create a long strip of matted paper to wrap around the album using a double fold on the sides to accommodate the width of the mini book. Overlap the strip in back and glue together to form a band that slides over the album to hold it closed.

9. Decorate the slider with a matted photo and matted eyelet word that is raised with foam adhesive to complete the mini book.

3

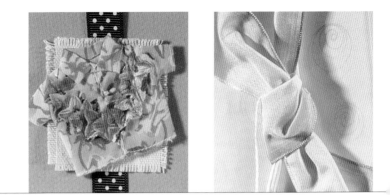

Fabric

DECORATING WITH
RIBBONS, FIBER, BUTTONS,
TRIMS, AND NOTIONS

More and more, the crafting lines are becoming blurred. Quilters are adding photographs to their heirloom-quality creations, and scrapbookers who flunked home economics in high school are now roaming the aisles at the local fabric store. As our page embellishments become more diverse, we are learning surprising new skills—such as threading a needle! Fabrics and notions are softer, gentler embellishments, and often give pages a homey, comfortable quality.

Working with notions can be as simple as gluing buttons onto a page, or as intricate as stitching a pocket or border directly onto the page. Small, portable sewing machines or hand-held machines are inexpensive and ideal for creating simple, basic stitches onto small page embellishments. I love working with beautiful ribbons—an elegant ribbon that matches the background paper makes a lovely addition to a wedding or baby page. Other notions, such

as lace, yarn, rickrack, twisted paper yarn, and raffia, make wonderful embellishments. Use fiber to create laces on die-cut shoes or to hang decorative elements, such as tags or charms.

Fabric can be used in place of patterned paper—it provides nice dimension without a lot of bulk. It's also fun to match fabric to an item of clothing that someone is wearing in a photograph. Most die-cutting machines will cut fabric and felt nicely so you can stitch titles and shapes onto your pages or cut out paper doll clothes for a realistic touch. Spray adhesive

works well when adhering fabric to a page, and you can also run fabric through an adhesive machine to make it self-adhesive. Whether you stitch or glue it on, fabric and notions will liven up your pages and provide soft, subtle dimension.

Karen

Maddie

Robert

The photos are labeled: play saucer • gymnast doll • Green Acres cookie jar • gymnast • carousel • tambourine • Lucky Ducks • Clifford the Big Red Dog • the telephone • headband • Sesame Street play swing • pager • Baby Blessings Bible • dancing sunflower • Polite Elephant book

Tag text: There are a few of my favorite things

Favorite things

Combine lots of photos that feature several different events with a theme, such as favorite things. All photos don't need to be scrapbooked chronologically. Page titles like "Favorite Things" can encompass photos that cover several years. If you are overwhelmed with tons of photos, this is a great way to start.

MATERIALS

patterned paper

card stock

ribbon

tag

adhesive

eyelet

eyelet
setting tool

paper punch

personal
computer

1. Punch photos into equal-sized squares and roughly lay out the photos, but do not attach them to the page.
2. Print journaling onto the background page.
3. Adhere photos onto the background page and mat onto a slightly larger contrasting colored paper.
4. Place the matted photos layout onto a larger piece of background paper in a coordinating color and pattern.
5. Tie a ribbon vertically along the left edge of the background paper to create a border and to support the title tag.
6. Place an eyelet through the hole in the tag and tie into the ribbon.

Elena and Nick's wedding day

Don't forget to check the upholstery section of your favorite fabric store when hunting for scrapbook embellishments. Decorative cording provides a distinctive and textural way to frame a picture.

1. Cut foam core into a 10" (25.4 cm) square block. Cut another square from the center, leaving 2" (5 cm) on all sides. The opening will be 8" (20.3 cm) square. Cut a scrap of foam core to the size of the photo and mount the photo onto it.

2. Add patterned paper to the foam core, cutting it to fit.

3. On the back of the foam core, add double-sided tape. Apply cording to the inside and outside edges of the foam core. Be sure to apply cording with the flange on the underside of the cording. On the outside edge, the flange will want to double onto itself at the corners; trim the overlap. On the inside edges, add a slit in the flange at the corner to allow the cording to bend smoothly around the corner. Be sure to keep the cording smooth and even by checking how it looks from the front.

4. Mount a 9" (22.9 cm) square of patterned paper onto the center of the coordinating patterned paper. Mount the foam core square over that, centering it on the page.

5. Cut Vs in the ends of the ribbon. Fold the edges to pleat as shown. (This is much easier with wire-edged ribbon.)

6. Mount the ribbon onto the page. Mount the journaling block onto the ribbon, and then mount the photo to the center of the page.

MATERIALS

patterned paper

ribbon

decorative cording

journaling block

foam core

double-sided tape

craft knife

DESIGNER: JENNA BEEGLE

embroidery floss

plain paper

die-cut tags

rubber stamps

ink pads

eyelets

eyelet setting tool

embroidery needle

paper punches

journaling marker

pencil

Home for the holidays

Hand embroidering a title on a scrapbook page adds
a homey feeling to a holiday page.

1. Use a pencil to write the word "home" in cursive. Use an embroidery needle to punch holes in the pattern over the word and embroider the greeting.

2. Stamp the words "for the" and "holidays" using red ink.

3. Create the tags for the page by stamping a small Christmas tree on each of the tags.

4. Layer the tags onto card stock and secure them with eyelets.

5. Add additional embellishments to the tags using paper-punched stars, buttons, and embroidery floss.

DESIGNER: SHELLI GARDNER

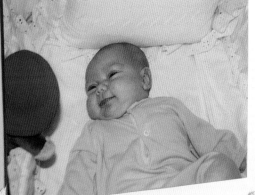

Who would Sarah give her first smile to? Would it be her beloved brother? Would it be her adoring mother? Would it be the father she had wrapped around her little finger?

One day when Sarah was about four weeks old, I heard her cooing for the first time. I snuck into her room, camera in tow, just in time to catch her smiling and talking to Paddington Bear! It was her first real smile!

DESIGNER: KELLY JONES

First smile

Multicolored letter beads strung from fiber make charming titles for scrapbook pages.

1. Print journaling on the upper left of the background paper and the lower right of the foreground paper.

2. Tear the foreground paper on the diagonal and place it over a portion of the background paper, making sure the journaling on both the background and foreground pages is visible.

3. Unravel a piece of acid-free twisted paper yarn, flatten it, and glue it down. Thread a coordinating color of fiber through various-sized buttons, knot the fiber, and glue the buttons down.

4. String multi-colored letter beads from coordinating fiber across the center of the page to draw the eye to both pictures.

5. Place three squares on the bottom to balance the layout and attach them to the page with tiny eyelets to keep the square from appearing ordinary.

MATERIALS

plain paper

acid-free twisted paper yarn

fiber

buttons

letter beads

glue

eyelets

eyelet setting tool

personal computer

MATERIALS

- plain paper
- canvas fabric
- ribbon
- 3-D stickers
- adhesive
- foam adhesive
- scissors
- pen
- eyelet letters
- eyelet setting tool
- die-cutting machine

Cancun

Enhance a scrapbook page with 3-D stickers that offer intricate detail featuring fabric, beads, foil, and more.

1. Start with turquoise and green 12" x 12" (30.5 cm x 30.5 cm) sheets of paper. Cut down the green paper and attach it to the turquoise along the right side of the page, leaving a small strip of turquoise exposed.

2. Run a piece of black-and-white dotted ribbon down the left side of the page. Attach the loose ends of the ribbon to the back of the page using tape.

3. Die-cut three squares out of canvas fabric. Fray the edges of each square and attach them, evenly spaced out, over the black-and-white ribbon. Add 3-D stickers to each fabric square.

4. Triple-mat each photograph using two shades of turquoise and black paper.

5. Arrange the photos on the green paper and add a journaling panel raised with foam adhesive for dimension.

6. Attach eyelet letters over two shades of turquoise paper to create a title for the page.

What Sarah is doing at seven months

Crawling around the house

Reading Board Books alone

Eating Cheerios by herself

What Sarah is doing at seven months

Fasten a bow to a page with Velcro, allowing the viewer to lift the bow and reveal the handwritten journaling behind the photo.

1. Cut three of the patterned papers to make quadrants on the other patterned paper and mount them.

2. Mount ribbon on the page between the quadrants.

3. Adhere a photo onto the card stock with ribbon corners.

4. Cut another piece of card stock the same width as the photo, but twice as long. Score it, fold it in half, and journal.

5. With the long piece of card stock closed, and the fold at the bottom, mount the photo to the folded card stock, sandwiching the tail of the hanging ribbon between the papers in the center. About 1" (2.5 cm) of ribbon and the bow will hang out at the top.

6. Mount this to the page, carefully lining up the bow with the ribbon on the page. Add a piece of Velcro to the back of the bow and to the ribbon on the page. Now, the Velcro will keep the card closed, but it can be opened by lifting the ribbon.

7. Add buttons with mini glue dots.

MATERIALS

patterned paper

ivory card stock

blue ribbon

blue bow

blue ribbon corners

ribbon

buttons, various sizes

adhesive

mini glue dots

Velcro

scissors

journaling pen

paper trimmer

MATERIALS

card stock

corrugated paper

vellum

ribbon

metal charm

adhesive

rubber stamps

ink pad

scissors

eyelets and
eyelet setting tool

paper punch

personal computer

Mimi & me

Corrugated paper combined with ribbon and
charms can help add dimension to a special photo.

1. Tear a strip of red paper vertically to create a border.

2. Punch photos using a square punch to create an accent border.

3. Cut corrugated paper lengthwise to create a visual stand on which the focus photo can rest. Wrap corrugated paper with coordinating ribbon, threading the charm through the ribbon before tying. Adhere the ribbon to the page.

4. Mat the photo onto card stock and then again onto the corrugated paper.

5. Punch a heart out of card stock.

6. Adhere a vellum subtitle over the heart using eyelets.

7. Stamp the title.

Charles Augustus Melville

Distinctive elegance is achieved on this heritage page by weaving ribbon through the background paper. Varying the width of the ribbon enhances the beauty.

1. Trim a sheet of background paper to 11 1/2" x 11 1/2" (29.2 cm x 29.2 cm).

2. Working on the back sides, determine the ribbon placement and lightly draw in ribbon outlines. Using a ruler for accurate placement, determine slits for the ribbon to weave through the paper. The slits are made in the same places for all four sides and for both sides of the ribbon. Cut slits with a craft knife.

3. Cut ribbon slightly more than 12" (30.5 cm) in length. This will allow extra ribbon in case it frays as it is woven. Weave the ribbon through the slits.

4. Use glue to hold the ends, adding a tiny bit of glue to the edge of the ribbon to prevent fraying.

5. Allow the ends of the narrow ribbon to extend beyond the edge of the paper.

6. Mount the paper by weaving it onto a second sheet of patterned paper. Adhere ribbon ends to that page.

7. Add a square of patterned vellum to the center of the page with ribbon corners. Trim the ribbon corners so that the underside does not show through the vellum.

8. Mount the photo and a journaling block.

MATERIALS

plain paper

patterned paper

vellum

ribbon

ribbon corners

glue

scissors

craft knife

ruler

personal computer

DESIGNER: JENNA BEEGLE

Charles Augustus Melville · October 1873

DESIGNER: CAROL RICE

MATERIALS

denim paper

card stock

two denim squares (one with pocket)

letter stickers

narrow strip stickers

snaps

audio recording device, such as the Memory Button

glue dots

eyelets and eyelet setting tool

die-cutting machine and dies

Pocket-full of treasure

Use denim on a scrapbook page and add new meaning to "Jeanealogy!" Turn a pair of worn-out jeans into a page by filling the pocket with photos, journaling, or treasured souvenirs.

1. Die-cut a button cover out of the corner of the pocket of a denim square.

2. Mount the denim squares onto a piece of card stock using star eyelets and snaps.

3. Accent the layout with narrow strip stickers in the corners.

4. Fold the denim paper into thirds and make a photo booklet by adhering the first two "pages" with snaps.

5. Insert the booklet into the pocket and adhere stickers.

6. Record a message on the audio recording device and cover with the denim die-cut button cover. Adhere the audio recording device with glue dots.

Lindsay Spero began babysitting McKenna and Payton in July of 2002 while Mommy would leave to teach her scrapbooking classes. I knew from the moment she interacted with the girls she would be terrific. So when I saw them sitting in McKenna's closet playing with the tub full of toys, I couldn't resist snapping this photo.

Miss Lindsay

Miss Lindsay

Using light colors with black-and-white photos creates visual interest on a page. A strip of ribbon across the page can soften the seam where the two papers meet.

1. Layer a piece of contrasting colored card stock over the bottom half of the background paper after printing the journaling on the computer.
2. Obscure the seam by covering it with a strip of ribbon.
3. Tie a separate ribbon bow and slide onto the ribbon strip.
4. Thread a tag through the bow's knot with embroidery floss.
5. Mat a photo in black.
6. To create a perfect bow that sits straight, tie the bow onto the ribbon strip after creating the bow.

MATERIALS

card stock
ribbon
embroidery floss
tag
adhesive
personal computer

Miss Lindsay

DESIGNER: CARA MARIANO

MATERIALS

plain paper

patterned paper

ribbon

gold press-on numbers

foam adhesive

glue dots

tape

scissors

die-cutting machine and dies

personal computer

Megan's sugar plum wishes

Ribbon comes in a large variety of colors and patterns, and it is a simple way to add texture and dimension to a scrapbook page.

1. Out of two shades of green paper, cut two rectangles—one slightly smaller than the other but the same width as the background page. Layer the two rectangles and position them at the top of the page to create a border.

2. Layer two different red ribbons over the green border. Attach the loose ends on the back of the scrapbook page using tape. Finish the border by adding a bow in the center.

3. Crop and mat a photograph as well as a title bar printed on the computer.

4. Die-cut gifts out of plain and patterned paper. Complete the gifts by adding red and green ribbon to each gift.

5. Attach the gifts along the bottom of the page. Use foam adhesive to create dimension.

6. Finish the page by adding a date with press-on numbers at the bottom of the green border.

Dear santa,
defihe
good.

It's the same story every year: Ashley always hems and
haws about going to see Santa, but once we get there,
she's thrilled to sit on his lap and tell him what she
wants. Sarah, on the other hand, is always eager to see
him BEFORE we got there, but when she finally gets
on his lap, she's a little intimidated. This year she was
actually stunned into silence!   Ashley, 9 and Sarah, 3

Dear Santa, define good

Decorate the seam where two textured papers meet with a
little glue and glitter. Popping up parts of your layout really
makes it stand out!

1. Place a die-cut tree on the bottom corner of paper and adorn with sequins
   for ornaments.
2. Place glue dots and silver glitter at random intervals near the top of the page.
3. Single-mat the photograph and adhere to the background paper. Place "Dear
   Santa" letter on the background paper, barely overlapping onto the photograph.
4. Place a journaling block below the photograph and adhere to the page with
   eyelets.
5. Choose coordinating paper and embellishments to create gifts.
6. Adhere gifts to the page, raising with foam adhesive for added dimension.

MATERIALS

patterned paper

journaling block

die-cuts

glitter

adhesive

foam adhesive

glue dots

eyelets

eyelet setting tool

personal computer

Model extraordinaire

Sheer fabric accents are a perfect complement to translucent vellum. Fabric flowers can be strategically placed to hide the vellum adhesive.

1. Select a background paper that coordinates with the colors in your photographs.
2. Evenly space photos on a solid band of coordinating colored card stock and place the band across the center of the layout.
3. Print the title on vellum, and then chalk and place at an angle to give a little dimension. Fasten fabric flowers on the ends of the title block to hide the glue spots under the vellum.
4. Select a few choice words that depict the moods of the child in the pictures and print the words on vellum.
5. Cut the words into circles and place them in round tags.
6. Punch a hole and string fiber through the holes to draw them together for a smooth flow.

MATERIALS

plain paper

card stock

vellum

fiber

tags

flowers

glue

scissors

chalk

hole punch

personal computer

A star is born

Color blocking is a wonderful way to highlight a special photograph. The simple use of two colors adds subtle style to the page. Connect the color blocked squares with ribbon.

1. Select two contrasting colors for the overall page layout.

2. Use the darker of the two colors for the background page, and then cut two squares, each equaling one-fourth the size of the background paper. On this page, the artist used 12" x 12" (30.5 cm x 30.5 cm) paper, so the contrasting squares are each 6" x 6" (15.2 cm x 15.2 cm).

3. Diagonally place the light squares onto the dark background page.

4. Hand-cut four stars—two dark and two light. Place one of the light stars near the top of the dark paper and fasten it to the page with a dark eyelet. Repeat this process for the right side of the page, using the opposite colors.

5. Place a dark star at the center of the page so that it lays half on the light side and half on the dark side. Cut the remaining light star in half (roughly) and set the light half on top of the dark half.

6. Anchor a ribbon on the center star and tuck the ribbon through each of the eyelets.

7. Place a photograph onto the background paper. Placing the photograph slightly off center adds more visual interest to the page.

8. Print journaling onto a sheet of vellum, tear the edges, and adhere the journaling block to the page.

9. Create the title from letter stickers and place above the stars.

DESIGNER: KELLY JONES

MATERIALS

plain paper

vellum

ribbon

journaling block

letter stickers

adhesive

scissors

eyelets and eyelet setting tool

personal computer

MATERIALS

card stock

vellum

fiber

vellum bubble stickers

liquid glaze

embossing powder

adhesive

rubber stamp

ink pad

watermark pen

chalk

eyelets and eyelet setting tool

heat tool

hole punch

personal computer

One fish, two fish, red fish, blue fish

Combine heat embossing with liquid glaze to create a dimensional title that is sure to make a big splash.

1. Print the page title on card stock and chalk inside the letters as desired. On top of the chalk, use a watermark pen and sprinkle embossing powder over the watermarked areas. Use a heat tool to emboss the letters.

2. Do a second layer of embossing by using liquid glaze over the paper to make the embossing powder bubble up and resemble water.

3. Tear three pieces of card stock horizontally in colors that are similar to the ones in the photograph.

4. Chalk the card stock as desired and place onto the background page. Stamp a few images along the bottom layer that coordinate with the images in the photograph.

5. Mount the photograph onto card stock, punch a hole in two corners, and thread the holes with several pieces of fiber that are knotted at the top to make it appear as if the picture is hanging.

6. Print the journaling on vellum and tack it down on the card stock at an angle. Then anchor the journaling into place with a vellum bubble sticker.

DESIGNER: KELLY JONES

Listen to Kayla make her "kitty" noises

Kitty Kayla

Record a child's voice on an audio recording device
and make scrapbook pages come alive with sound.

1. Die-cut the title, mount it onto the background paper, and make a title box.

2. Adhere the box to the background page.

3. Mount and attach the photographs with snaps.

4. Make accent boxes using snaps or ribbon and apply patches in a coordinating theme.

5. Paint the audio recording device using a sponge applicator and an archival stamp pad.

6. Record a message on the audio recording device and decorate it with a kitty patch. Adhere the kitty patch to the audio recording device with glue dots.

7. Print text squares on vellum and adhere them to the page with spray adhesive.

MATERIALS

plain paper

patterned paper

vellum

small fabric patches

ribbon

snaps

audio recording device, such as the Memory Button

spray adhesive

glue dots

sponge applicator

archival ink pad

die-cutting machine and dies

personal computer

Summer fun keepsake box

MATERIALS

plain paper or
card stock

ribbon

sun die-cuts

foam adhesive

double-sided tape

eyelet numbers

eyelet punch

hammer

die-cutting
machine and
dies

A gift box is the perfect place to store photos from a particular
event or occasion. Whether the box is die-cut or recycled from a
previous birthday, it is decorated using the same tools and supplies
as a scrapbook page. Connecting the lid and the photos with ribbon
creates a 3-D display the moment the lid is lifted. Leave the box
out for visitors to view and kiss your coffee-table books goodbye!

1. Die-cut a box that will accommodate the size of your photos. The placement
   of the box decorations will be dictated by whether the photos are horizontal
   or vertical.

2. Poke a hole in the center of the box lid with an eyelet punch. Thread ribbon
   through the hole, taping one end to the top of the lid and leaving the remainder
   of the ribbon long enough to position all of your photos. (Half of the photos
   are on one side and half are on the back side.)

3. Decorate the box top with a
   colored band, the title, and
   eyelet numbers to designate
   the year. The sun die-cut is
   raised with foam adhesive.
   The colored band will effectively
   cover the hole and the ribbon.

4. Mat each photo on larger
   paper, leaving room to label
   each one. One paper can
   be left without a photo for
   journaling.

5. The matted photos are sand-
   wiched together in pairs with
   a ribbon in the middle, leaving
   almost 1" (2.5 cm) of ribbon
   exposed in between to allow
   accordion folding of the photos.

6. Accordion fold the photos and
   place them inside the box so
   that when the lid is lifted the
   photos will begin to lift out
   of the box.

DESIGNER: SANDI GENOVESE

4

Metal

WORKING WITH WIRE, EYELETS, FOIL, SNAPS, MESH, CHARMS, AND CHAIN

It sounds unbelievable, doesn't it? Adhering metal objects onto paper that you intend to last for generations. Well, applied correctly, small metal objects won't cause any harm to your pages; but they will add sparkle to your layouts and functionality to your design elements. Best of all, many manufacturers have taken extra measures to make metal embellishments scrapbook-friendly.

Eyelets have become a new staple in scrapbook supplies. They not only add a decorative touch, but they also are used to attach items such as tags and labels to a page. I like to use them to dangle die-cuts and charms from ribbon, which adds movement to pages. Eyelets are available in all sorts of colors, shapes, and sizes. You need a hole punch, an eyelet setter, and a hammer to attach some brands, while others simply snap onto your page. Brads offer a similar functionality and flair.

Gold and silver beaded metal chain, which has been commonly used on key rings, is one of my favorite metal embellishments. I use it to outline die-cuts, photos, or mats, and it's amazing how much vibrancy and pop it adds to my pages. It is particularly striking when used against black background paper. Wire is another fun material to add to your pages, and it comes in a range of colors and gauges. Wrap it around letters or die-cuts or form it into curvaceous borders.

Foils, charms, metal tags, snaps, mesh, washers, paper clips—you name it. The most utilitarian household item can become a dazzling scrapbook embellishment. If you use the appropriate adhesive and keep an eye out for sharp edges, your heavy metal pages should offer long-lasting glimmer and enjoyment.

Girlfriends

Some metallic embellishments look like pewter and are perfect to enhance black-and-white photos. When adding ribbon to a layout, it's fun to attach it so that it looks loose and free.

1. Trim purple card stock ⅛" (3 mm) on all sides and adhere to maize card stock.
2. Trim vellum ¾" (1.9 cm) larger than the large photo on the right side of the page.
3. Trim maize card stock ⅛" (3 mm) larger than vellum and mat behind the vellum.
4. Adhere the large photo to the vellum.
5. Adhere photo corners to the corners of the vellum using glue dots.
6. Cut small pictures to fit three charm frames and place them inside the frames.
7. Using satin ribbon behind them, arrange the frames at the bottom of the page with glue dots to adhere the frames to the ribbon.
8. Trim three small pieces of vellum matting on maize card stock trimmed 1/16" (1.5 mm) larger than vellum.
9. Set three eyelet words to each matted piece of vellum.
10. Adhere metal "girlfriends" word with small glue dots at an angle in the left corner of the page.
11. Place the eyelet words—one beneath another—below "girlfriends."

MATERIALS

card stock

vellum

satin ribbon

charm photo corners

charm frames

metal words

adhesive

medium glue dots

eyelet words and eyelet setting tool

Camp Arrowhead

Create hand-looped photo holders from wire to embrace vintage photographs.

1. Mount an 11" x 11" (27.9 cm x 27.9 cm) square of patterned paper onto black background paper.

2. Layer a 10" x 10" (25.4 cm x 25.4 cm) square of vellum and four strips of black stripe, wrapping the strips around to the back of the background page.

3. Make the bottom ribbon with a 2" (5 cm) strip of green patterned paper, two black ribbon strips, and two 1/2" (1.3 cm) strips of floral patterned paper.

4. Form small loops at the ends of 8" (20.3 cm) of 20-gauge wire. Wrap around a 1" (2.5 cm) circular item to form the holder.

5. Mount the pictures in die-cut frames and mat them in green and black paper.

MATERIALS

plain paper

patterned paper

vellum

20-gauge wire

die-cut frames

adhesive

paper trimmer

DESIGNER: JENNIFER MASON

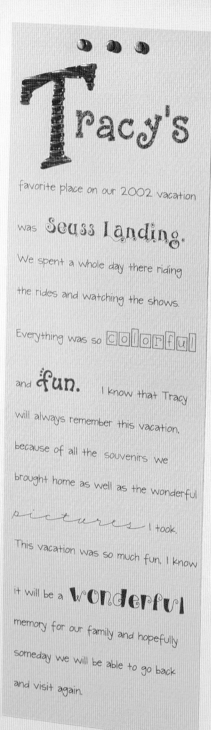

Tracy's

favorite place on our 2002 vacation

was **Seuss Landing.**

We spent a whole day there riding

the rides and watching the shows.

Everything was so colorful

and **fun.**   I know that Tracy

will always remember this vacation,

because of all the souvenirs we

brought home as well as the wonderful

pictures I took.

This vacation was so much fun. I know

it will be a **wonderful**

memory for our family and hopefully

someday we will be able to go back

and visit again.

Seuss Landing

Seuss Landing

Decorative foil is a lightweight, soft, pliable metal, which is easy to cut and use to add texture. Combine it with a photograph to add a special gleam to any scrapbook page.

1. Start with a yellow 12" x 12" (30.5 cm x 30.5 cm) background page.

2. Die-cut the first letter of the person's name out of red decorative foil. Run the letter through a crimper to get a wavy texture.

3. On the computer, print out a story for the page. The top of the story should be the person's name, but make sure to leave off the first letter—it will be replaced with the one made of foil.

4. Place the finished journaling panel on the far left side of the page. Add three red brads to the top of the panel. Punch holes out of red decorative foil the same size as the brads and attach the circles onto the brads.

5. Double-mat a photograph in two shades of red paper and attach to the page.

6. Die-cut three squares out of blue decorative foil. Turn the foil squares over and place them on a soft surface like a mouse pad. Take a stylus tool and create a decorative design in the foil. When the squares are turned over, they will look embossed.

7. Attach the three finished squares under the picture using foam adhesive to create dimension.

8. Hand-cut three wavy designs. Run the cut pieces through a crimper to create texture. Attach the waves at the bottom of the page. Place three brads underneath each wave. Add foil circles over each brad.

9. On the computer, print out a title and mat it using two shades of red paper.

MATERIALS

plain paper

patterned paper

decorative foil

brads

adhesive

foam adhesive

scissors

stylus

paper crimper

paper punches

die-cutting machine and dies

personal computer

MATERIALS

card stock

24-gauge wire, nontarnish silver

beads

nail heads

adhesive

paper crimper

paper trimmer

die-cutting machine and dies

Kirstin at the park

Dimension is fundamental with the addition of wire to a scrapbook page. Bend it, twist it, and crimp it for various looks.

1. Add the beads to the wire. Bend and twist the wire to spell out the title.

2. Adhere the title card stock and add nail heads for dots on the letters.

3. Mat the photographs.

4. Die-cut three tags in contrasting colors of card stock.

5. Bend the wire to form flower petals and adhere to the card stock with nail heads.

6. Crimp the wire and thread it through the tags. Adhere the tags to the page.

Our family Christmas

Combine upper and lower case letters to spell out page titles for a less symmetrical look. Colored eyelets are a nice touch when combined with silver-colored metal frames.

MATERIALS

- striped paper
- card stock
- alphabet charms
- metal words
- glue dots
- eyelet words and eyelet setting tool

1. Trim striped paper ¼" (6 mm) on all sides.
2. Don't adhere to the hunter green card stock until the eyelet word "family" has been set.
3. Triple-mat a family photo on celery green, hunter, and off-white card stock.
4. Trim 1 ½" (3.8 cm) squares from celery card stock and mat on brick red card stock, tearing around all edges of the brick card stock.
5. Using a small glue dot, adhere holiday charms on each of the four squares.
6. Using two glue dots on each letter to spell "our," center the alphabet charms in the upper center of the page.
7. Set the eyelet word "family" under "our" through the back of the striped paper. Adhere the striped paper to the hunter paper, creating a mat.
8. Place a family photo in the center.
9. Back the tag with hunter card stock and set four eyelets in each corner of the tag (through the card stock).
10. Set the words "Merry Christmas" eyelet in the middle of the tag on hunter card stock.
11. Adhere the completed tag with glue dots.

DESIGNER: JULIE LARSEN

plain paper

decorative foil

decorative
wood frames

wire

die-cuts

adhesive

foam adhesive

alphabet letter
stamps

ink pads

craft knife

silver pen

hole punch

die-cutting machine
and dies

personal computer

Amanda and Dennis

Decorative wooden frames painted with gold
metallic paint add an elegant touch to festive
photographs for a memorable holiday page.

1. Start with a red 12" x 12" (30.5 cm x 30.5 cm) paper for the background.

2. Crop photos to fit inside decorative frames. Make small wire rings to connect
   the frames together. Punch holes in each picture and attach wire rings.

3. Die-cut ornaments out of decorative green and gold foil. With a craft knife, cut
   away detail.

4. Connect all the frames and the ornament together with gold wire rings and
   attach them to the left side of the scrapbook page.

5. Die-cut holly out of three shades of green paper. Add detail to each holly leaf
   with a silver pen.

6. Double mat a photograph with green and metallic gold paper. Arrange the picture
   on the page. Attach the holly leaves around the picture and the page. Use foam
   adhesive to add dimension.

7. On the computer, create a journaling block on metallic gold paper. Add completed
   holly leaves on the bottom corner.

8. Create a title with alphabet letter stamps and holly stickers.

DESIGNER: CARA MARIANO

One of Landon's Easter eggs from Grandma and Grandpa promised him a **t r i p t o t h e z o o**, so Memorial Day weekend we decided to call them on it. We all made the 3 hour drive to the closest zoo in St. Louis. The kids really enjoyed seeing all of the animals and our family had a great time together.

DESIGNER: DONNA DOWNEY

Zoo

Go a little wild when selecting dimensional elements for your scrapbook pages. The wire elephant on this page is actually a paper clip found at an import store.

1. Crop photographs into six equal squares and mount them onto solid-colored card stock.
2. Cut a hole in another piece of card stock and use foam adhesive to set mounted pictures behind it to create an inset window.
3. Use fiber to thread through a dated bookplate and foam adhesive to hold it in place.
4. Stitch an elephant paper clip to the page using embroidery floss and use the clip to hold the journaling block in place.

MATERIALS

card stock
fiber
embroidery floss
bookplate
journaling block
elephant paper clip
foam adhesive
glue dots
tape
scissors

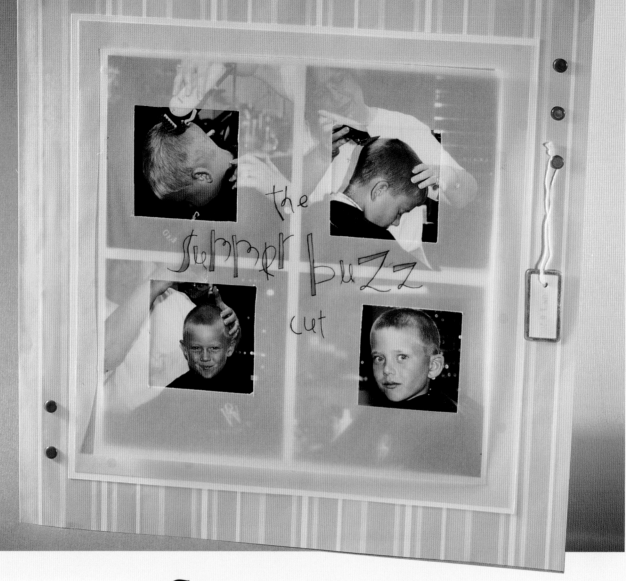

MATERIALS

patterned paper

card stock

vellum

ribbon

tag

snaps

vellum adhesive

date stamp

ink pad

craft knife

pencil

colored pencils

paper punch

personal computer

The summer buzz cut

Cut squares out of plain vellum paper and fasten over the top of photos creating "see-through" mats that focus your attention on the subject of the photos.

1. Crop photos and center them on polka-dotted background paper. Mount the polka-dotted page onto a contrasting colored solid page.

2. Place the single-matted layout onto a larger striped piece of paper.

3. Cut vellum slightly larger than the photos. Place the vellum over the pictures so that there is a small border extending beyond the photos.

4. Punch a square out of scrap vellum. Place the square over the desired window and trace it with a pencil. Cut out the windows using a craft knife.

5. Practice writing a freehand title on plain computer paper. When the desired look is achieved, trace it onto vellum and shade in using colored pencils.

6. Adhere the vellum over the photographs with vellum adhesive.

7. Stamp a small tag with a date that relates to the photographs.

8. Add snaps to the layout, using one of the snaps to hold the date-stamped tag in place.

Siblings

Combine the straight edges of photographs and wire mesh with the torn edges of vellum for a unique layout.

1. Cut a strip of wire mesh to fit along the left side of the page.

2. Place a black-and-white picture somewhat centered on the page, barely overlapping the mesh.

3. Print the title and journaling on vellum and tear and chalk the edges in a coordinating color.

4. Place the title on the upper right side of the page and the journaling on the bottom left side.

5. Use eyelets to make the kids' names and attach them to the bottom right of the picture.

MATERIALS

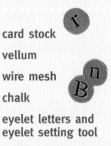

card stock

vellum

wire mesh

chalk

eyelet letters and
eyelet setting tool

personal computer

DESIGNER: KELLY JONES

My Wish

I often sit
and wish that I

Could be a kite
up in the sky.

Ride upon the wind
and go.

Whichever way
I chanced to blow.

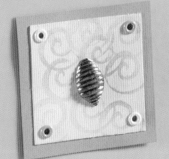

My wish

Bronze charms fastened to rubber stamped paper squares add dimensionality to ocean-themed pages. Rubber stamped swirls mimic the feeling of water within each paper square.

1. Select two coordinating card stocks. Tear the foreground card stock in half horizontally and adhere it to the background card stock.

2. For the title, string fiber through two tags, and attach the fiber on either end of the layout through eyelets.

3. Put a letter sticker on the first tag and tack it down with mini glue dots. Finish the rest of the word with a watermark pen, simulating the letter sticker, and then chalk in shades that coordinate with the torn foreground paper. Repeat for the second word of the title.

4. Mat the photograph in a color that will make the subject stand out.

5. Print the journaling (in this case a poem) on vellum. Tear it, chalk the edges, and tack it down to the page.

6. To balance the layout, cut three squares of complementary colored card stock, and layer with a contrasting, trimmed piece of card stock.

7. Stamp a design on the smaller piece of card stock with a watermark pen and then chalk in the same colors as the title.

8. Add seashell charms to the stamped pieces of card stock, tying the squares in with the picture, and attach them with tiny white eyelets.

MATERIALS

card stock

vellum

fiber

stickers

vellum tags

seashell charms

glue dots

watermark pen

chalk

eyelets and eyelet setting tool

personal computer

DESIGNER: KELLY JONES

MATERIALS

card stock

vellum

fiber

embroidery floss

poetry tags

buttons

scissors

craft knife

eyelets and eyelet setting tool

personal computer

Sassy

Tags are a wonderful way to make a journaling block or title take center stage on a page.

1. Print a title on vellum and adhere to card stock of a contrasting color from the background page.

2. Cut the title into the shape of a tag, allowing portions of the letters to hang over the edges of the tag. Trim excess vellum with a craft knife in the space between the top and bottom of overhanging letters and the edge of the tag.

3. Attach an eyelet to the hole in the top of the tag and string contrasting colored fiber through the hole. Attach poetry tags to the ends of the fiber and place the tag on the page.

4. Mat the picture and place it at an angle for a different look.

5. Journal on vellum and cut it into strips, attaching strips with threaded buttons at intersecting corners.

Carnival

Create the look of a photo within a photo by printing an extra copy, cropping a small piece and raising it with foam adhesive before attaching it to the "parent" photo.

1. Create a graphic background by using perpendicular strips of contrasting card stock.
2. Place the focal point photo within the large strip of card stock.
3. Place photos on the second page within the other two strips.
4. Crop a double print of the photos to focus on action and mount on foam adhesive.
5. Use eyelet letters to create the title.

MATERIALS

card stock

foam adhesive

eyelet letters and eyelet setting tool

paper punch

MATERIALS

card stock

vellum

ribbon

fiber

charms

adhesive

glue dots

cotton balls

watermark pen

chalk

eyelets and eyelet setting tool

paper punch

personal computer

That first day

Create a charming page combining ribbon and silver charms.

1. Print the titles on white card stock and frame them by threading ribbon into eyelets placed on the top and bottom of the title boxes.

2. Mat photographs, leaving an approximate 1" (2.5 cm) border on the top only. Punch two holes on the top section, approximately 1" (2.5 cm) apart, centering them. Thread ribbon through the holes, leaving enough ribbon to run the length of the mat.

3. Print journaling blocks and then trim. Place a watermark pen line around the boxes and go over with chalk on a cotton ball.

4. Highlight some of the charms by framing them with vellum tags, and "hanging" them from the pictures, using fine fiber. Attach charms to the tags with small glue dots.

Ski Utah

Create stunning three-dimensional snowflakes
using a rubber stamp, embossing powder, and a heat tool.

1. To create the 3-D snowflakes, pour a small pile of embossing powder directly onto the card stock. Carefully hold the card stock in the air without spilling the powder and hold the heat tool beneath the card stock so the powder will melt without blowing away.

2. As soon as the powder is melted, put the card stock down and press the stamp into the liquid powder. Allow it to set for 10 to 15 seconds, then remove the stamp.

3. Place the photos and layer vellum on top, leaving a space for part of the photograph to show through. Mount vellum to the page with mini deco fasteners.

4. Stamp title letters onto white tags and fasten them to the page with mini deco fasteners.

5. Die-cut a snowflake and embellish with snowflake-printed vellum. Add journaling to the vellum.

MATERIALS

plain paper

card stock

patterned vellum

tags

die-cut snowflake

mini deco fasteners

rubber stamps

ink pad, watermark

embossing powder

journaling pen

paper punch

heat tool

DESIGNER: SHELLI GARDNER

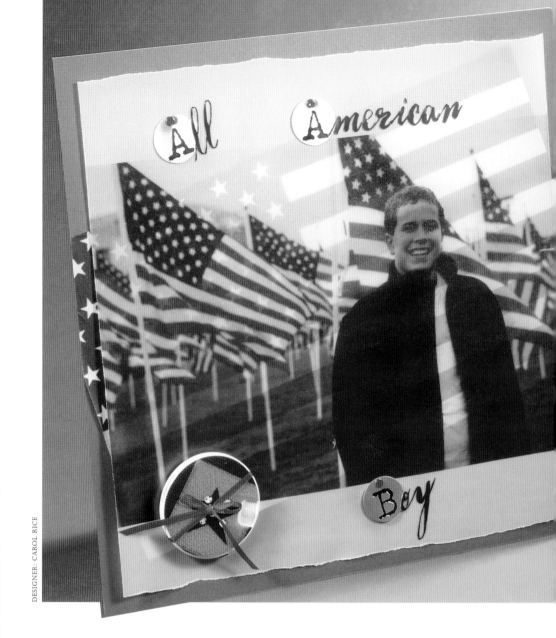

DESIGNER: CAROL RICE

MATERIALS

card stock

vellum

ribbon

flag (memorabilia)

letter tags

letter stickers

audio recording
device, such as the
Memory Button

die-cut audio
recording device
cover

snaps

spray adhesive

glue dots

eyelet setting
tool

die-cutting
machine

All American boy

Metal letter tags are a great way to give a title
added dimension.

1. Mount the fabric flag onto the card stock.

2. Color copy a photo onto vellum. Tear the edges and mount on top of the flag.

3. Adhere letter tags with snaps using an eyelet setting tool.

4. Apply stickers to complete the title.

5. Record a patriotic song, scout oath, and so forth, on the audio recording device.

6. Color copy a patriotic sticker onto vellum and die-cut the button cover.

7. Adhere the button cover over the audio recording device with spray adhesive, tie
a ribbon, and adhere the audio recording device to the page with glue dots.

Rebecca Carter Colefax

Create the illusion of a lacy border to separate patterned papers with colored eyelets. The eyelet holes allow the colored paper sitting behind them to peek through for a dramatic, two-toned effect.

1. Trim a sheet of patterned paper to 10" (25.4 cm) square. Trim a sheet of contrasting patterned paper to 11 ¾" (29.8 cm) square. Mount the smaller square of paper onto the larger square.

2. Using a ruler for guidance, add eyelets along the edge between these two papers, staggering the rows of eyelets.

3. Cut a piece of coordinating patterned paper as a mat for the photo and mount it using eyelets.

4. Cut a sheet of coordinating patterned paper twice as long as the top block. Cut the same size of plain vellum and card stock. Line all the pieces of vellum, patterned paper, and card stock together and fold in half. Punch two ³⁄₁₆" (4.8 mm) holes for eyelets near the fold line.

5. Punch matching holes where the booklet will be placed and above the booklet's fold line in the background paper. Add eyelets to all holes. Thread ribbon through the holes, going down through the booklet and up through the page above it. Tie off the ribbon and cut Vs into the ends.

6. Mount the whole page onto a sheet of coordinating patterned paper, leaving a thin edge of contrasting colored border.

DESIGNER: JENNA BEEGLE

Hearty mini memory book

A handmade mini memory book makes a perfect gift for friends and family. While this one is themed with a heart trimmed with beaded metal chain, the theme can be adapted for any special event by simply changing the color scheme and cover decoration.

1. The book's spine is a black strip of paper 24" x 6" (61 cm x 15.2 cm). The first and last fold create the front and back cover at 3 ¼" (8.3 cm). The inside is accordion folded with each pleat measuring 1 ¾" (4.4 cm) (for a total of five pleats).

2. Cut two red covers each measuring 6" x 8" (15.2 cm x 20.3 cm) and attach them to the inside of the front and the back black covers.

3. Cut four additional red sheets to 6" x 8" (15.2 cm x 20.3 cm) and attach one to each of the inside pleats.

4. To hold the pages together, place red ribbon along the inside of the back cover, around the bottom of all the pleats, and up along the inside front cover. Tie a bow at the top.

5. To decorate the front cover, die-cut a red heart and fasten it to a square of sheet adhesive (with the exposed adhesive facing up).

6. Snake gold beaded metal chain along the perimeter of the heart in three rows, using wire snips to cut the chain in the cleavage and at the tip.

7. Use scissors to trim the adhesive flush with the ball chain.

8. Remove the protective backing from the heart back and attach the decorated heart to a black square matted in gold.

9. Raise the square with foam adhesive and attach to the album's front cover.

MATERIALS

plain paper
or card stock

ribbon

heart die-cut

gold beaded
metal chain

sheet adhesive

foam adhesive

scissors

wire snips

5

Keepsakes

USING SOUVENIRS, MEMENTOS, DRIED FLOWERS, SEASHELLS, AND AUDIO RECORDING DEVICES

A lock of hair from your baby's first hair cut. Dried flowers from your bridal bouquet. The key to your first sports car (in my dreams!). Keepsakes from big moments in your life can bring back a memory like no other 3-D embellishment. And, if they aren't too big and bulky, they can find a home on a scrapbook page.

Oftentimes, a keepsake is safest when placed in a clear, acid-free keepsake envelope or pocket. But items such as postcards, menus, invitations, cards, concert tickets, and stamps can be directly adhered to a page. If an item, like a road map or a college degree, is too large for your page, stick it in the color photocopier and reduce it down to a manageable size, or enlarge it to become a background element on the page. Keepsake items can also serve as decorative elements. Extra fabric or beading from a wedding gown can create an elegant border. A tassel from a graduation

cap can dangle from a page title. Birthday candles can be pieced together to form letters in a celebratory title.

Thanks to the wonders of technology, you can now incorporate sound into your pages. Small, flat audio recording devices, such as the Memory Button, enable you to record sound—like a child singing a favorite song—and attach it to your page for a lifetime of listening pleasure.

Hearing a person's voice can conjure up all sorts of emotions. I'll never forget one such instance when I was taping a segment of a scrapbooking television program that I host. My guest had incorporated the audio recording device in her layout of her father talking to his granddaughter. I didn't even know these people, and I started getting all choked up as I listened to the message. I asked the director to do another take, and I got all choked up the second time—even though I knew it was coming! It just goes to show that keepsakes—both real and virtual— can be powerful additions to your scrapbook pages.

McKenna & Payton
Myrtle Beach
May 2002

As they greet the beach they hold out their hand
And I watch them scoop tiny handfuls of sand
A look of pure wonder washes over each face
On the edge of the blanket they sit in one place
Wiggling their toes and having such fun
As they enjoy the day and bask in the sun.

the beach
explorers
summer '02

The beach explorers

This project uses seven layers of complementary patterned paper that are trimmed progressively smaller. Build the foam core section first and then adhere it to the background page to create a shadow box that will protect the seashells.

1. Cut a piece of foam core smaller than your background paper and wrap it with patterned paper, like a gift. The one we show is 10" x 10" (25.4 cm x 25.4 cm).

2. Adhere a second piece of slightly smaller patterned paper over the first layer on the foam core.

3. Cut a rectangle window on the left side of the foam core using a craft knife.

4. Cut a piece of patterned vellum to fit the open space on the foam core, large enough to show a mat around the photographs, and adhere to the foam core.

5. Mount the two larger photos on the vellum.

6. Attach smaller, framed photos, thread together with complementary colored ribbon, and add the title tag.

7. Raise small photos with foam adhesive.

8. Line the back of the rectangle with complementary patterned paper, drill holes in seashells, and thread ribbon through. Fasten the ribbon to the back of the foam core.

9. Cut another piece of complementary patterned paper slightly larger than the rectangle and attach it to the back of the foam core to anchor the ribbon in place.

10. Double mat the foam core onto two pieces of patterned paper in coordinating colors.

MATERIALS

patterned paper

patterned vellum

silk ribbon

die-cut frames

four seashells

foam core

foam adhesive

craft knife

drill

DESIGNER: JENNIFER MASON

Roses

DESIGNER: KELLY JONES

MATERIALS

card stock

fabric roses

dried baby's breath

adhesive

paper punch

personal computer

Document a special anniversary by including dried flowers from the special event.

1. Select the background card stock.
2. Place photographs and journaling block in a geometric fashion onto the card stock.
3. Anchor the journaling block to the page with fabric roses at each corner.
4. Fill in empty spaces with geometric shapes containing words that pertain to the pictures.
5. Select a prominent empty space to place dried flowers from the bouquet.

Love

Warmth   Joy

Soul

Mate

For the first time in 22 years of marriage, we were separated on our anniversary. Danny sent me this beautiful bouquet of roses. 4-25-02

Balboa Island

Incorporate found objects such as seashells and sand
on layouts with the use of embossing powder.

1. Make background paper for the square accents by using several scrap pieces of coordinating card stock. Run the paper through an adhesive machine to apply adhesive to the back. Randomly tear and cut the paper into strips. Press the strips onto a coordinating background sheet.

2. Randomly stamp on top of the paper.

3. Mix sand with transparent embossing powder. Use a paintbrush to randomly apply white glue to the paper. Sprinkle the sand and embossing powder mixture onto the glue and shake off the excess. Heat to emboss.

4. After the glue has dried, die-cut squares from random spots on the newly created paper.

5. Trim around the outside of the square hole to create a frame for the squares.

6. Add shells to the squares with glue.

7. Apply the squares to the inside of the frames using foam adhesive to raise them.

8. Apply sand and seashells to the tags using the sand and embossing powder mixture and the same technique.

9. Highlight a focus photo by mounting a 4" x 6" (10.2 cm x 15.2 cm) print to a duplicate 5" x 7" (12.7 cm x 17.8 cm) print with foam adhesive.

MATERIALS

- card stock
- tags
- sand
- seashells
- embossing powder
- foam adhesive
- white glue
- rubber stamps
- ink pad
- scissors
- paintbrush
- adhesive machine, such as a Xyron
- die-cutting machine and dies
- heat tool

July 19, 2002

MATERIALS

card stock

vellum

ribbon

fabric hearts

drawstring bag

audio recording
device, such as the
Memory Button

adhesive

glue dots

hole punch

Our love

Place a keepsake item, such as an audio recording
device, in a sheer bag on a scrapbook page to cleverly
conceal the audio element.

1. Trim the edges of the vellum and adhere to the card stock.

2. Mount a photo on card stock, punch a hole and thread ribbon through,
   and mount the silver heart in the center.

3. Record a love song, vows, and so forth, on an audio recording device and
   slip it into a silver drawstring bag.

4. Adhere the drawstring bag and ribbons to the page using glue dots.

5. Adhere the silver hearts over the knots of ribbon.

Myrtle Beach

Souvenirs like seashells collected on vacation set the mood for a beach page. If your shell collecting was not successful, you can purchase beach embellishments like shells, starfish, and sand dollars.

1. Tear sand-colored card stock to create a sand border.
2. Mat the focus photo in coordinating blue paper.
3. Create the journal tag. On the page shown, the letters that spell "beach" were pulled out of the journaling.
4. Thread three shades of coordinating embroidery floss through the hole in the tag. Chalk and mat on coordinating blue card stock.
5. Chalk the title and "bury" in the sand.
6. Adhere shell, sand dollar, and starfish to create the beach feel.

MATERIALS

- plain paper
- card stock
- embroidery floss
- handmade tag
- seashells
- adhesive
- chalk

A day at the circus

Create dimensionality on scrapbook pages with souvenirs such as ticket stubs and programs. Additional dimension can be added by layering stickers with foam adhesive. Layering is made simple by neutralizing the adhesive on the back of stickers with baby powder.

1. Apply blue polka-dot stickers around the outside edge of the page. Apply red-checkered stickers around the whole page, just inside the border of blue dots.

2. Cut along the mouth of the giraffe sticker and insert one end of the gold thread underneath, leaving about 1" (2.5 cm) dangling. Add the giraffe to the bottom of the page, standing on the checkered line. Tape the other end of the gold thread to form a tightrope wire. Adhere the photo to cover the end of the wire. Add two yellow star stickers back-to-back on the end of the dangling "wire" to keep it from unraveling. Make a star necklace and add a hat sticker for the giraffe.

3. Add the cycling bear sticker to the tightrope wire. Add mounting tape to the back of the umbrella sticker leaving the protective layer in place. Powder the open umbrella only, to neutralize the adhesive. Remove the protective paper and place the umbrella in the bear's hand. Glue the tickets together, add some mounting tape to them to give them dimension, and slip them under the bear's other hand.

4. Cut one side of the blue striped square from a geometric sticker to match the curve in the elephant's back, and add it to create a blanket. Trim the square with a red and gold striped sticker, a silver star sticker, and a small purple star sticker. Add the elephant sticker to the parade, overlapping the giraffe slightly in order to create dimension. Add a party hat sticker and a monkey balancing a ball.

5. Add the circus elephant leaning against the rear of the lead elephant. Pop a large lollipop sticker with mounting tape and tuck it under the trunk. Add a crown sticker.

6. Pop the pink cotton candy sticker, put it in the hand of the dressed dog sticker, and add it to the parade.

7. End the parade with the juggling monkey sticker and some ball stickers.

8. Add red sliver stickers to mat the photo.

9. Trim the title from the circus program, attach above the photo, and trim with sliver stickers.

DESIGNER: SHERYL UMLI

MATERIALS

plain paper

gold thread

stickers

baby powder

tape

glue

scissors

MATERIALS

plain paper or
card stock

patterned paper

vellum

thread

beads

adhesive

foam adhesive

double-sided tape

scissors

pencil

ruler

creasing tool

pre-cut die-cuts
or die-cutting
machine and dies

"I do" nesting keepsake boxes

Nesting boxes provide a unique way to enjoy your photos and
store souvenirs. This is a grouping of seven boxes, each one
slightly smaller than the next. Three-dimensional souvenirs—
like a champagne cork—that are too thick to include on a
scrapbook page can be placed inside the smallest box.

1. To make the largest box lid, begin with paper or card stock that measures
   12" x 12" (30.5 cm x 30.5 cm). With a ruler and a pencil, draw an X from corner
   to corner on the back side of the paper (Figure A).

2. Fold in each corner to the middle of the box, which is the intersection of the X
   (Figure B). Use a creasing tool to make crisp folds. (Figure C).

3. Fold in the corners again, this time so that they touch the first fold lines (Figure D).

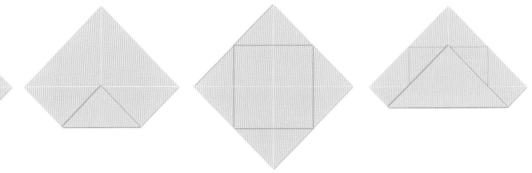

Figure A	Figure B	Figure C	Figure D

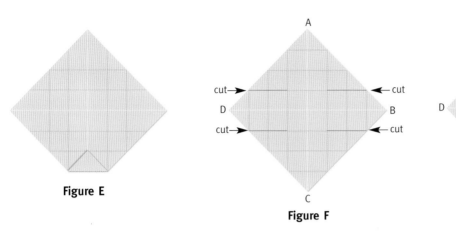

Figure E

Figure F

Figure G

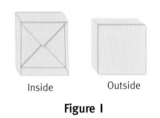

Figure H

Inside   Outside

Figure I

4. Fold the corners again, so that they touch the closest fold lines (Figure E).

5. Cut along two side folds, stopping at the fold that indicates the top of the box (Figure F).

6. Position corners B and D so they are on the sides with corners A and C as the top and bottom. Fold in corner C so that it touches the penciled X in the center and use double-sided tape to hold it in place (Figure G). Bring up the box side, reinforce the fold line, and swing in the arms that will become the other two sides (Figure G).

7. Repeat this step with the corner directly opposite (Figure H).

8. Bring in corner D, trapping the side arms underneath, and stick to the inside with double-sided tape.

DESIGNER: SANDI GENOVESE

9. Repeat with opposite side corners (Figure I).

10. The box bottom is made in the same way, beginning with a square that is 11 ³/₄" x 11 ³/₄" (29.8 cm x 29.8 cm). Each successive box (lids and bottoms) will be ¹/₄" (6 mm) smaller than the preceding box. For a fit that is not quite as snug, use ¹/₂" (1.3 cm) between each box (lids and bottoms) instead of ¹/₄" (6 mm).

11. After building all fourteen boxes (seven lids and seven bottoms) add photos, journaling, and themed die-cuts to each of the box lids. Place souvenirs inside the final, smallest box. (Photos are matted and attached to box lids. Die-cuts and punches are raised with foam adhesive, sometimes in multiple layers. Beads are strung onto thread and wrapped around heart die-cuts.)

12. When all of the boxes are nested inside each other, cut a vellum strip to wrap around the outside box and decorate the strip with a matted eyelet word. If you can't locate vellum that is long enough, attach each end to a square of coordinating paper that will sit on the bottom of the nested boxes.

6

Beads & Baubles

DESIGNING WITH BEADS, MIRROR, SEA GLASS, GLASS PEBBLES, GLITTER, TURQUOISE, AND RHINESTONES

As I'm designing my pages, I sometimes feel like I'm regressing into my childhood. Discovering an object that I can incorporate into a layout brings out an exhilarating excitement. As I look at the layouts in this chapter, I remember cherishing objects, such as pieces of smooth sea glass and beaded friendship bracelets, as a young girl, and I get just as excited seeing them used in scrapbook pages. Besides giving these pages dimension, shine, and color, they add a nice dose of sentimentality.

Scrapbook stores now carry beads, word pebbles, mosaic tiles, and glass do-dads in all sorts of shapes and colors—many of which are self-adhesive. Did you ever think you'd be making Shrinky Dinks after the age of ten? Think again, because they are popping up on pages faster than you can turn on the oven. I like to die-cut shrink film, rough it up with sandpaper, rubber stamp an image, and add detail with chalks and colored pencils. Once baked,

the film shrinks down to about one-eighth its original size and the color really intensifies, leaving you with a small, vividly detailed embellishment, customized for your layout.

For a completely overwhelming experience, visit a local bead store. The variety of beads will be staggering, but you are guaranteed to find just what you need to accessorize your layout. Even mass-consumer stores are starting to carry poetry beads and other 3-D embellishments. Who knows? You could be wandering the aisles looking for toilet paper and discover the perfect scrapbook treasure.

Megan, our little princess

Beads add new dimension to a scrapbook page and are available in an endless assortment of colors and textures that makes it very easy to coordinate with any theme.

MATERIALS

plain paper

patterned paper

thread

heart charm

beads

adhesive

foam adhesive

die-cutting
machine and dies

personal computer

1. Cut a 12" x 12" (30.5 cm x 30.5 cm) piece of patterned paper down to 8 ½" x 12" (21.6 cm x 30.5 cm). On the computer, create the journaling and run the trimmed paper through the printer. Attach the printed paper onto a solid colored 12" x 12" (30.5 cm x 30.5 cm) page leaving the solid color exposed along the right side.

2. Crop and mat photographs and arrange around the journaling. Print a title on the computer and attach it to the page.

3. Die-cut flowers out of two shades of pink paper. Cut away detail on the lighter pink flower and layer onto the darker pink flower. Place a small amount of strong adhesive tape in the center of each flower. Sprinkle beads over the tape and press with your finger to create the center of each flower.

4. Die-cut leaves out of green patterned paper.

5. Arrange the leaves and completed flowers along the left side of the page. Add foam adhesive to some of the flowers to create dimension.

6. Print a title on the computer on two lines. Separate the two lines, and apply a strip of strong adhesive to the top and bottom of the first title line. Add beads to the tape. Finish by stringing a gold heart charm and beads on thread that hang from the bottom of the second title line.

Lowry Park Zoo

Glass beads add a certain sparkle and dimension to a page without much effort.

1. Dip a small paintbrush into glue and paint the glue into the biggest circles on the patterned paper.

2. Pour glass beads into the circles and swish them around, making sure all of the glue is covered. Use a craft knife to carefully edge around the circle, loosening all of the excess beads.

3. Gently shake off the excess glass beads onto a paper plate and pour them back into a bead container. Let the glue dry overnight to harden and give the circles a finished look that won't distract the eye from the beautiful paper.

4. Center a photograph on the top half of the paper between the circles and the edge.

5. Create the page title with stickers on vellum. Tear the vellum into squares and use a fine marker to edge around the letters so they stand out.

6. On the right page, punch out focal parts of some photos, glue them onto the page, and then cut out squares to frame them. Raise them with foam adhesive.

7. Double-mat the remaining photographs and place them on the page.

8. Print journaling onto vellum, and then cut to resemble the circles on the left page.

MATERIALS

plain paper

patterned paper

card stock

vellum

letter stickers

glass beads

foam adhesive

glue

scissors

craft knife

journaling pen

fine marker

paintbrush

paper punch

personal computer

Beads & Baubles 84·85

DESIGNER: KELLY JONES

Westchase Elementary's first grade class went on a field trip to Lowry Park Zoo. Allie Banales and Sarah rode the merry-go-round (laughing the whole time), petted the stingrays in their pool (surprised at how soft and smooth they were), and were amazed at the size of some of the fish in the big tanks (bigger than our house)! They also loved watching the manatees with their sweet faces, but the best part was having lunch under the covered canopy.

Lowry Park Zoo

Ronald Letrick

Many patterned papers look just like fabric. A paper "ribbon" trimmed from a larger sheet appears dimensional but lays perfectly flat and partners well with fabric ribbon and word beads.

MATERIALS

plain paper

patterned paper

black ribbon, ³/₈" (1 cm) wide

platinum ribbon, ⁷/₈" (2.2 cm) wide

platinum ribbon corners

tag

word beads

adhesive

glue

scissors

1. Frame a square of striped paper (the one we show is 9 ³/₄" [24.8 cm] square) with four strips of ribbon and miter the corners. (The ribbon strips are created by trimming the edges from a coordinating patterned paper.)

2. Place the framed paper onto a larger sheet of coordinating patterned paper.

3. Mount the large photograph with photo corners to a mat that is slightly larger than the photograph. Mat a second time, leaving a larger border along the bottom of the photograph.

4. Mount the small photograph to a mat that is slightly larger than the photograph. Mat a second time, leaving a larger border along the bottom of the photograph.

5. Lace two beads with 9" (22.9 cm) and 6" (15.2 cm) pieces of black ribbon, tie a knot on the right side of the bead, trim the ends, and glue the threaded beads onto the mats.

6. Layer a solid colored journaling block onto coordinating patterned paper. Wrap the matted journaling block with ⁷/₈" (2.2 cm)-wide ribbon and the bead laced with black ribbon, knotted on both sides and trimmed. Mount onto a larger piece of solid paper and adhere to the page.

7. Hand-cut two flower clusters from patterned paper, adhere to the page, and place a small tag on top with the person's name.

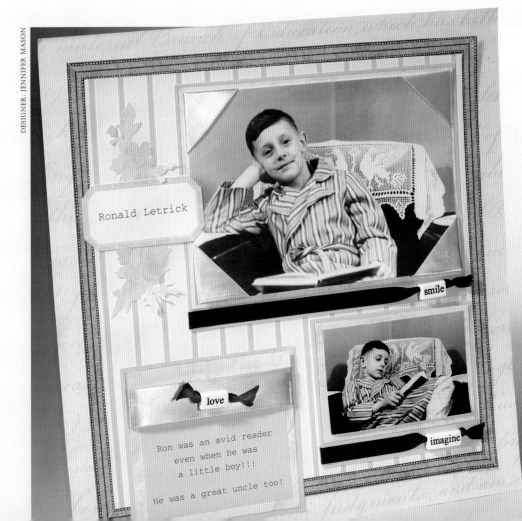

DESIGNER: JENNIFER MASON

Ronald Letrick

smile

love

imagine

Ron was an avid reader even when he was a little boy!!!

He was a great uncle too!

DESIGNER: STEPHANIE BARNARD

Kirstin

Dimension and texture come together when wire
and beads are added to handmade paper accents.

1. Add beads to wire, tying knots in various places, and wrap the beads around the photo.

2. Triple-mat the photo, leaving room in the second mat to add a stamped title.

3. Using glue dots, add mirrors next to the title.

4. Dip a sea sponge into a watermark ink pad and stamp onto the background card stock.

5. Adhere the photo to the layout.

6. Add beads to wire, tying knots in various places, and wrap around the background card stock.

7. Die-cut hearts out of handmade paper.

8. Wrap the hearts with the beaded wire and adhere to the layout.

MATERIALS

handmade paper
card stock
black 26-gauge wire
beads
mirrors
adhesive
glue dots
sea sponge
rubber stamps
ink pad, watermark
black ink
paper trimmer
die-cutting machine and heart dies

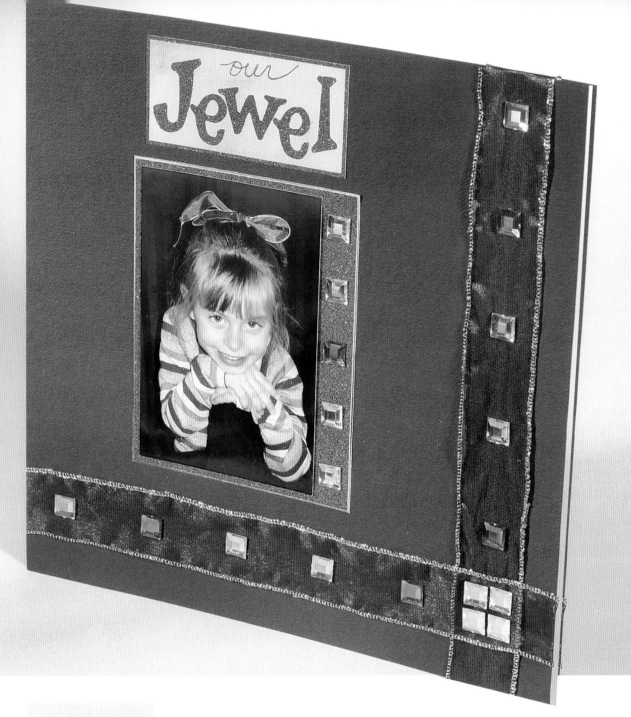

MATERIALS

plain paper

iridescent-coated paper

card stock

ribbon

jewels

adhesive

glue dots

die-cutting machine and dies

Our jewel

Jewels and ribbon add delight and charm to a layout. Complement a child's smile with jewel embellishments along with the actual ribbon worn in the photo.

1. Die-cut the title and adhere it to gold paper and iridescent-coated paper.
2. Add ribbon to the layout.
3. Mat the photographs with gold and purple iridescent-coated paper.
4. Add jewels to the ribbon and photo mat using glue dots.

Simple sweet moments

Glass pebbles are a fun way to highlight little details
on a scrapbook page.

MATERIALS

1. For the background, layer yellow paper on top of gold paper that has been
   cut slightly larger to create a border.

2. Die-cut the title out of red paper using the lollipop alphabet. Layer the letters
   onto orange paper and cut around them to create a small border. For variety,
   leave some letters on an orange rectangle instead of cutting around them.

3. Die-cut hearts out of a variety of colors. Layer the hearts onto a strip of red
   paper and position the paper at the bottom of the page, raising some with
   foam adhesive. Add highlights with a silver pen.

4. Crop and mat a photograph with red and orange paper.

5. Punch tiny hearts out of a variety of colors. Place a clear pebble over the
   hearts and position it on the page.

6. Journal around the pebbles to complete the page.

plain paper

clear pebbles

foam adhesive

silver pen

paper punch

die-cutting
machine and dies

DESIGNER: CARA MARIANO

DESIGNER: BECKY WHALEY-BUTLER

MATERIALS

card stock

organza ribbon

wire

glitter

glue pen

scissors

die-cutting
machine and dies

Christmas card photo shoot

Add sparkle to any page by adding glitter to ribbon and wire.

1. Tear a strip from the top and bottom of the background card stock.

2. Place a piece of red organza ribbon in the space left by tearing out the strip
   and back it with white card stock.

3. Die-cut Christmas lights from red and black card stock. Trim the top from the
   red light and adhere it to the black light. Highlight the lights by using a glue pen
   to fill in the highlight area on the red bulb. Sprinkle red glitter on the glue and
   shake off the excess.

4. String the lights on wire and attach it to the top of the page.

5. Use a glue pen and glitter to highlight the mat for the focus photo.

DESIGNER: E.L. SMITH

Free standing sandstone rock up to 1,000 feet tall create a truly magical desert landscape.

Utah

Turquoise beads enhance the look of these southwestern photographs, but the mood is set with the watercolored background. Although the paper is flat, the watercolor layers create the feeling of dimensionality and set the tone for the entire layout.

1. Create the background page by layering watercolor washes. Start with a light color and add more paint as you layer to create dimension.

2. Paint 6" x 6" (15.2 cm x 15.2 cm) swatches of coordinating colors to use for die-cutting.

3. Die-cut three rectangle frames from black paper. Die-cut three zigzag frames out of the color coordinated watercolor swatches and position over the black frame.

4. Attach photos to the backs of the frames.

5. Die-cut two suns and embellish with watercolor circles. Place the suns on the page.

6. Title the page using die-cut letters.

7. Journal along the curves.

8. To finish, attach a string of turquoise stones with an aggressive adhesive.

MATERIALS

plain paper

watercolor paper

turquoise stones

adhesive

watercolor paint

journaling pen

paintbrush

pre-cut die-cuts or die-cutting machine and dies

At the ripe old age of 16, Brandon thought he was too old for Santa! He did agree to dress in a red shirt like his sisters so I could get a picture, but I didn't even suggest that he sit on his lap OR tell him what he wanted for Christmas (money). I wanted to take the kids shopping afterwards, but they refused to walk through the mall with their matching shirts on. We settled on lunch instead! Dec. 2001

DESIGNER: KELLY JONES

You're never too old for Santa

Replicate the look of strings of Christmas lights with brightly colored beads that decorate a journaling card.

MATERIALS

card stock

vellum

wire

beads

adhesive

foam adhesive

eyelets and eyelet setting tool

paper punch

personal computer

1. Use a paper punch to cut out three evenly spaced trees from the bottom of the layout, and place a coordinating color of card stock behind the trees.

2. Type the title on vellum. Create the title bar by cutting textured card stock and mounting it onto the background page.

3. Place the vellum title on the far right side of the title bar. On the left side, adhere one of the punched trees to the textured card stock with foam adhesive.

4. Mat the picture with a thin border and place on the same card stock used behind the trees, making sure to cover the width of the layout, but also leaving a small border on either side.

5. Type the journaling on vellum and attach the vellum to the card stock with eyelets.

6. String the beads on wire, alternating the main colors in the layout, and tuck the extra wire behind the layout through eyelets.

Bubbles

The transparent quality of vellum and glass beads help to re-create the look of bubbles on a page. Attaching vellum to a less-than-perfect photograph with eyelets softens the image and takes focus off the photo underneath.

1. Select the background paper. Select coordinating paper and trim approximately ¹/₂" (1.3 cm) all the way around.

2. Place a horizontal strip of mesh along the bottom quarter of the page. Embellish the mesh with stickers that relate to the photographs.

3. Cover one photograph with vellum and attach it to the photograph with eyelets at each corner.

4. Double-mat the other photograph and adhere both photographs to the page.

5. Mount the journaling block on top of the mesh, raising it with foam adhesive for added dimension.

6. Run vellum through an adhesive machine and cut title letters from it using a lettering template. Chalk letters lightly before adhering to the page. (Placing adhesive on the back of the vellum will cloud the transparent quality of the vellum, allowing greater visibility of the letters on the background page.)

7. Embellish the page with a few more stickers, overlapping the photographs for visual interest.

MATERIALS

card stock

vellum

mesh

watch crystal

stickers

adhesive

foam adhesive

chalk

eyelets and eyelet setting tool

lettering template

adhesive machine, such as a Xyron

DESIGNER: KELLY JONES

Beaded heart album page

Use special water-based lacquers to achieve a transparent raised
coating that results in a truly three-dimensional finish.

MATERIALS

plain paper

card stock

journaling banners

photo corners

micro beads

embossing ink
and powders

water-based
lacquer

adhesive

scissors

white correction
pen

heat tool

stamping mat and
back-up paper

cleaning tray
and rag

rubber stamps

spray bottle and
water for clean up

1. Rubber stamp hearts and emboss on card stock using embossing ink and powder.
   Cut out the outlines, leaving small paper edges.

2. Apply a layer of water-based lacquer in one open area of the design at a time.
   Shake micro beads over the wet lacquer and shake the excess back into the jar.
   Allow to dry at least 30 minutes. Repeat with a second coat of beads.

3. Apply a smaller amount of water-based lacquer over part of the design for shading
   or accent, and apply a second color of micro beads. Allow to dry thoroughly.

4. Rubber stamp photo corners and banners, then emboss them using embossing
   ink and powder. Cut them out, leaving small paper edges.

5. Apply a contrasting color of 8 ½" x 11" (21.6 cm x 27.9 cm) paper to the
   left side of 12" x 12" (30.5 cm x 30.5 cm) background paper.

6. Apply photo corners to the smaller page, mat photos, arrange, and adhere
   into place.

7. Journal in banners with white correction pen, arrange the journaling around
   the photos, and adhere into place.

8. Arrange heart stickers along the right side, scatter around the photos, and
   adhere into place.

DESIGNER: DEE GRUENIG

Pisces

Iron-on rhinestones are an easy way to add color and glimmer to any scrapbook page. They iron onto paper just as easily as they do onto fabric or can be fastened with adhesive.

1. On 12" x 12" (30.5 cm x 30.5 cm) black paper, arrange the rhinestone alphabet letters at the top of the page and iron them onto the paper.

2. Underneath the title, arrange a design using metallic silver iron-on decorations. Once the design is what you want, iron it onto the paper.

3. Mat a photograph in red paper and attach it to the page. Draw a border around the photograph using a silver pen.

4. Die-cut squares out of silver decorative foil. On the computer, print on vellum paper the words that will go on the squares. The vellum will help in the placement and transfer of the words.

5. Place the foil on a soft surface, such as a mouse pad, and use a stylus tool over the vellum to transfer the letters onto the foil. Remember to transfer the words backwards so when the foil is turned over it will read the right way.

6. Attach the finished foil squares to the page using red brads.

MATERIALS

plain paper

vellum

decorative foil

iron-on rhinestone alphabet

iron-on metallic silver decorations

brads

silver pen

stylus

die-cutting machine and dies

iron

personal computer

Best buds

Create a mini book for a special friend that is sure to become a keepsake. This mini book can have more or less pages, based on your preference, and can be altered to fit any occasion by changing the colors and embellishments. The checkered pattern of the book pages creates visual interest even before the pages have been decorated.

MATERIALS

plain paper

textured paper

patterned paper

thread

alphabet beads

brads

clear page protector

adhesive

foam adhesive

adhesive machine, such as a Xyron

pre-cut die-cuts or die-cutting machine and dies

paper trimmer

personal binding system with discs

1. Select three sheets of four different colors of paper (for a total of twelve sheets) and arrange them in a repeating pattern for the inside pages.

2. Trim the first two colors (pink and green) to 8 $\frac{1}{4}$" x 3" (21 cm x 7.6 cm).

3. Trim the next two colors (yellow and blue) to 8 $\frac{1}{4}$" x 3 $\frac{3}{4}$" (21 cm x 9.5 cm).

4. Continue to trim the remaining colors in batches of two, each $\frac{3}{4}$" (1.9 cm) taller than the previous batch. The final pages will be 8 $\frac{1}{4}$" x 7" (21 cm x 17.8 cm).

5. Trim $\frac{3}{4}$" (1.9 cm) from the length of every other color beginning with the first sheet (pink). When all are trimmed, you will have created a wonderful checkerboard pattern along the edge of the book. To vary the pattern, trim an additional $\frac{1}{8}$" (3 mm) from the width of every other page beginning with the first page (pink).

6. Cut a front and back cover 8 $\frac{1}{4}$" x 7" (21 cm x 17.8 cm) from dusty pink paper or card stock. Mat a square of patterned paper and center it on the front cover. Attach a die-cut heart from textured paper and adhere it with foam adhesive to the matted square. String alphabet beads onto thread to create the title and attach to the cover with colored brads. (Adhesive can be used on the back side of the beads to make sure they stay in place.)

7. Trim a clear page protector 8 ¼" x 7" (21 cm x 17.8 cm) to fit over the front cover for protection.

8. Using the personal binding system with discs, punch holes in the left edge a few sheets at a time. The bottom of each sheet should always butt against the guide on the cutting tool. The clear page protector and front and back covers should also be punched.

9. Insert the discs into the punched holes.

10. Add photos, embellishments, and journaling to inside pages.

7

Exotic Elements

CREATING ACCENTS WITH FEATHERS, LEAVES, CLAY, RAFFIA, WOOD PAPER, AND TWIGS

Sometimes a gift from Mother Nature is just the thing to accent a layout. Pages that center on outdoor activities, such as a trip to the beach, a camping excursion, or a layout of your garden in full bloom, benefit nicely from the addition of natural elements. A seashell, feather, or a pressed flower can make a special memory even more vivid.

As funny as it sounds, you can actually purchase many natural elements, such as those listed above. Or, you can pick up a souvenir from the beach or the trail, clean it, and carefully add it to your layout. Shells can be glued directly to a page or tucked into a keepsake envelope. Other natural items, such as leather and cork, can be decorated, pierced, and cut to create decorative elements. Fragile dried or pressed flowers should be protected in an envelope or behind a page protector.

Clay is a fun material to work with and embellish. Polymer clay is available in many different colors, and you can

create your own by blending colors. After the clay is baked, it is neutralized and won't harm your pages. I like to create clay tags and use letter stamps to impress single words that complement my layouts. You can also make your own beads from polymer clay. (Don't forget to poke holes in the clay beads before you cook them if you plan to hang them.) Enjoy these layouts courtesy of Mother Nature.

DESIGNER: GRACE TAORMINA

MATERIALS

card stock

raffia paper

dictionary page

photo corners

bronze wire

hemp twine

small envelope
and mailing tag
die cuts

cellophane window
mailing tag

wood beads

assorted
pressed leaves,
feathers, twigs,
and buttons

glue dots

rubber stamps

ink pads

scissors

colored pencils

grommet tools
and grommets

die-cutting
machine and dies

Nature walk

Sometimes nature is the best source for embellishments. The title
bar on this page is suspended from a twig collected on a walk.

1. Stamp the title and cut it into a rectangular shape. Add two grommets to the top,
   then set aside.

2. Die-cut a small envelope and glue three flaps together to form an open envelope.

3. Stamp a title on the envelope, and then stamp a few coordinating images along-
   side the envelope title. Set aside.

4. Glue a dictionary page onto card stock and die-cut it into a tag. Glue a pressed
   leaf to the front of the die-cut tag. Loop hemp twine through the hole and add
   a couple of wood beads. Set aside.

5. Glue an additional pressed leaf on the inside of the cellophane window mailing
   tag. Loop natural hemp at the hole.

6. Mount a photo onto a piece of card stock. Trim around the photo to create a
   deckle-edged border.

7. Stamp a few coordinating images onto the scrapbook page, shading with colored
   pencils as desired.

8. Add two pairs of grommets to the right top of the page. Position the grommets to
   accommodate the width of a twig. Use bronze wire to secure the branch to the page.

9. Loop hemp twine through the rectangular title label and tie it onto the branch.

10. Glue the mounted photo to the page with photo corners.

11. Use glue dots to adhere additional embellishments, such as the pressed leaf
    in the cellophane window mailing tag, rust-colored raffia paper, buttons, and
    additional pressed leaves.

Glenn and Cara

Explore the versatility and beauty of polymer clay with unique finishing, shaping, baking, and molding techniques.

1. Double-mat a photograph using colored corrugated paper and red handmade paper. Add decorative wire across the edges of the photograph and mats.

2. Place the finished picture on a black 12" x 12" (30.5 cm x 30.5 cm) background page.

3. Soften and roll out a piece of polymer clay and cut it into a square. Stamp names into the clay using alphabet stamps and punch a circle at the top so it can be hung. Stamp a heart into another piece of clay. Cut out the heart with a small circle cookie cutter or large pen cap. Repeat this three more times. Bake the square and circles according to polymer clay instructions.

4. After the clay is cool, arrange the circles with hearts onto small gold squares and attach to the background page.

5. Add four red eyelets underneath the photograph. Weave gold ribbon through the eyelets. Hang the finished clay square with the names from the ribbon and tie it in a bow.

6. Add a journaling square and gold circles around the page to create a finished look.

MATERIALS

plain paper

decorative handmade paper

corrugated paper

ribbon

decorative wire

polymer clay

foam adhesive

glue dots

alphabet stamps

rubber stamps

small circle cutter

eyelets and eyelet setting tool

paper punches

DESIGNER: CARA MARIANO

First signs of fall

plain paper

card stock

raffia

twine

adhesive

chalk

Combine raffia, torn paper, and twine for a rustic
effect reminiscent of a fall day.

1. Trim ½" (1.3 cm) on all four sides of background paper and mat onto
   contrasting card stock to create the frame.
2. Gather raffia to create a cornstalk effect and tie with twine.
3. Tear and chalk orange card stock to create the pumpkin.
4. Double-mat a photograph using two complementary colors of card stock.

DESIGNER: DONNA DOWNEY

first signs of fall

every year daddy excitedly decorates the
front yard and stoop for fall. the day
daddy puts up the cornstalks and
positions the bail of hay is our family's
first sign of fall

McKenna, October 2001

DESIGNER: SHELLI GARDNER

It's a jungle out there

Give added emphasis to a journaling box by matting it on a stamped background that has been "stitched" with raffia.

1. Randomly stamp flowers onto card stock with watermark ink, emboss with clear embossing powder, and let cool. Repeat this process on another piece of card stock for individual flowers and the title piece to cut out later.

2. Stipple over the embossed papers with coordinating ink colors, and then buff with a paper towel to blend colors and take off excess ink.

3. Stamp the page title onto the extra piece of embossed paper, emboss with clear embossing powder, triple-mat, and adhere to the page. Place a translucent feather over the title.

4. Stamp the remaining title words, cut out, mat, and then mount to the background paper.

5. Cut out separate flowers, single-mat some and embellish some flower centers with raffia, raising some off the page with foam adhesive.

6. Cut a journaling block from coordinating card stock, stamp a border along the top edge with watermark ink, and emboss with clear embossing powder. Stitch raffia over part of the stamped border. Journal onto coordinating paper, trim, and mount to the journaling block.

7. Mat photos and adorn corners of two photos with raffia.

MATERIALS

card stock

raffia

translucent feather

adhesive

foam adhesive

clear embossing powder

rubber stamps

ink pads, watermark

scissors

journaling pen

stipple brushes

paper towel

heat tool

you never really leave a place you love . . .

A place I love

Bring the feeling of the outdoors into your scrapbook with the addition of wood paper, which can give the illusion of dimension, especially when it is trimmed away and layered on a coordinating page.

1. Trim along the edge of the twig pattern with a craft knife. Place and adhere leaf paper with the twig overlapping the edge.

2. Double-mat the photo using contrasting card stock. Mount the matted photo to wood paper leaving an approximate 3" (7.6 cm) margin to the right.

3. Using glue dots on the back side, adhere wire across the face of the photo.

4. Mount buttons by using a hole punch and then threading wire and twisting over the top of the button. Place buttons in the top and bottom squares.

5. Record on the audio recording device a saying or nature sounds from a CD or other source.

6. Sponge colored ink onto the audio recording device. Decorate the button with wire coil and a button. Mount the coil and the button with a glue dot in the center of the audio recording device. Adhere the audio recording device to the page using glue dots.

7. Write the title heading along the left edge of the paper.

MATERIALS

twig paper

leaf paper

wood paper, such as Paperwood

card stock

brown craft wire

red buttons

audio recording device, such as the Memory Button

glue dots

craft knife

sponge

hole punch

Love guest book

paper

vellum

gold foil

twig

elastic hair band

adhesive

removable white
tape

brass stencil

hole punch

paper trimmer

adhesive machine,
such as a Xyron

die-cutting
machine and dies

personal computer

To emboss is to raise the design on the paper and is traditionally achieved with a brass stencil and stylus. Faux embossing involves cutting the design out of paper that matches the background and using adhesive to stick it on top. This guest book features circles and rectangles that have been adhered to the matching paper used for the cover, making it look embossed, but with a lot less time and effort than embossing the traditional way. The theme of the book can be altered by deleting the wedding information from the inside pages.

1. Cut the cover and inside pages to the desired size. The one pictured is 11" x 8 $\frac{1}{2}$" (27.9 cm x 21.6 cm). Judge the quantity of pages you will need by the amount of guests coming to the wedding. The front and back covers are lined with a slightly darker color to add interest and thickness. Punch two holes in the book. Base the distance between the holes on the length of the band that will be used for the binding.

2. Run paper through an adhesive machine to add an adhesive backing.

3. Create pairs of each rectangle by die-cutting or using the paper trimmer to cut strips that are $\frac{1}{4}$" x 1" (6 mm x 2.5 cm). Use die-cuts or craft punches to create pairs of circles in multiple sizes. Remove the backing from the top shape and stick to the matching circle or rectangle to double the thickness of each shape.

4. Use removable $\frac{3}{8}$" (1 cm)-wide white tape on the bottom and top of the front cover for a guide to position the rectangles to create stripes. Use loose rectangles of a different color as "placeholders" to accurately position each rectangle. (Placeholders are not fastened to the cover. They are only used as an aid to create stripes that are straight and evenly spaced.)

5. Randomly scatter the circles on the remainder of the cover.

6. Run a rectangle of gold foil an adhesive machine to add adhesive. Emboss the word "love" with a brass stencil. Multi-mat the embossed foil using varying shades of cream and tan.

7. For the inside pages, select a font and print the date, signature lines, and wedding couple's names on the computer.

8. The first sheet is a photograph of the wedding couple that has been photocopied on vellum.

9. Punch holes in the vellum and inside sheets that align with the cover holes.

10. Attach the matted embossed "love" to the cover. To complete the album, go to the hair accessory section of your local store and choose an elastic hair band in a coordinating color. Poke the elastic band through the top hole in the book. Insert a twig through the elastic band to hold the band in place. Stretch the band along the back cover and bring the other end of the band up through the remaining hole. Slide the other end of the twig through the elastic band and center the twig.

DESIGNER: SANDI GENOVESE

Love

Guests

Steve & Sarah · June 15, 2002

Resources

3M
(888) 364-3577
www.mmm.com
adhesives

Anna Griffin, Inc.
733 Lambert Drive
Atlanta, GA 30324
(404) 817-8170
www.annagriffin.com
paper, ribbon, vellum

Artistic Wire, Ltd.
752 North Larch Avenue
Elmhurst, IL 60126
(630) 530-7567
www.artisticwire.com
wire

Bazzill Basics
451 East Juanita Avenue
Suite 10
Mesa, AZ 85204
(480) 558-8557
www.bazzillbasics.com
paper

C-Thru Ruler Company
Sharon Ann Collection
6 Britton Drive
Bloomfiled, CT 06002
(800) 243-8419
www.cthruruler.com
paper

Canson
21 Industrial Drive
South Hadley, MA 01075
(413) 538-9250
www.canson-us.com
paper

Colorbök
2716 Baker Road
Dexter, MI 48130
(800) 366-4660
www.colorbok.com
David Walker stickers

Creating Keepsakes
14901 South Heritage Crest
Bluffdale, UT 84065
(801) 495-7230
www.creatingkeepsakes.com
computer fonts

Deluxe Cuts
P.O. Box 8283
Mesa, AZ 85214
(480) 497-9005
www.deluxecuts.com
laser die-cuts

Design Originals
2425 Cullen Street
Fort Worth, TX 76107
(800) 877-7820
www.d-originals.com
paper

DMC
(888) 610-1250
www.dmc-usa.com
embroidery floss

DMD Industries
2300 South Old Missouri Road
Springdale, AR 72764
(501) 750-8929
www.dmdind.com
paper

EK Success
P.O. Box 1141
Clifton, NJ 07014-1141
800-524-1349
www.eksuccess.com
zig pens

Ellison Craft & Design
25862 Commercecentre Drive
Lake Forest, CA 92630-8804
(800) 253-2238
www.ellison.com
die-cutting equipment, die-cuts, wood paper, Rotatrim paper trimmer, decorative foil, beaded metal chain, and Rollabind binding system

Emagination Crafts, Inc.
463 West Wrightwood Avenue
Elmhurst, IL 60126
(630) 833-9521
www.emaginationcrafts.com
paper punches

Fiskars
7811 West Stewart Avenue
Warsaw, WI 54401
(800) 950-0203
www.Fiskars.com
paper crimpers, paper punches, paper trimmers, scissors

Glue Dots International
5575 South Westridge Drive
New Berlin, WI 53151
www.gluedots.com
adhesives

JewelCraft, LLC
505 Winsor Drive
Secaucus, NJ 07094
(856) 374-1234
www.jewelcraft.biz
beads, wire, glass, mirrors

Jolee's Boutique
EK Success
P.O. Box 1141
Clifton, NJ 07014-1141
www.eksuccess.com
stickers

Karen Foster Designs
P.O. Box 738
Farmington, UT 84025
(801) 451-9779
www.karenfosterdesign.com
paper

Keeping Memories Alive
260 North Main
Spanish Fork, Ut 84660
(800) 419-4949
www.scrapbooks.com
paper (Cottage Collection)

Magenta Style
www.Magentarubberstamps.com
paper

Magic Scraps
1232 Exchange Drive
Richardson, TX 75081
(972) 238-1838
www.magicscraps.com
beads, buttons, seashells, mesh

Making Memories
1168 West 500 North
Centerville, UT 84014
(801) 294-0430
www.makingmemories.com
adhesives, brads, eyelets, letter tags, mini deco fasteners, paper, raffia, snaps, Twistel

Mary Engelbreit Studios
6900 Delmar Boulevard
St. Louis, MO 63130
(314) 726-5646
www.maryengelbreit.com
stickers

Mary Uchida
3535 Del Amo Boulevard
Torrance, CA 90503
(800) 541-5877
www.uchida.com
paper punches

Me and My BIG Ideas
30152 Esperanza Parkway
Rancho Santa Margarita, CA 92688
www.meandmybigideas.com
stickers

Memory Technology, Inc.
32 E. Red Pine Drive
Alpine, UT 84004
(801) 756-6194
www.memorybutton.com
memory buttons

Mrs. Grossman's Paper Company
3810 Cypress Drive
Petaluma, CA 94954
(800) 457-4570
www.mrsgrossmans.com
stickers, foam adhesive

Offray
Berwick Offray LLC
9th and Bomboy Lane
Berwick, PA 18603
(800) 327-0350
www.berwickindustries.com
ribbon

Paper Adventures
901 South 5th Street
Milwaukee, WI 53204
(800) 727-0699
www.paperadventures.com
paper, vellum (Parchlucent)

Paper Patch
8325 South 4300 West
West Jordan, UT 84088
(800) 397-2737
www.paperpatch.com
paper

Pier 1 Imports
www.pier1.com
elephant paper clip

Plaid Enterprises
P.O. Box 2835
Norcross, GA 30091
(800) 842-4197
www.Plaidonline.com
All Night Media pop dots,
foam adhesive, raffia,
rubber stamps

Posh Impressions
22600-A Lambert Street
Suite 706
Lake Forest, CA 92630
(800) 421-7674
www.poshimpressions.com
ink pads, rubber stamps

Provo Craft
151 East 3450 North
Spanish Fork, UT 84660
(800) 937-7686
www.provocraft.com
bradlets, paper, stickers

PSX Designs
360 Sutton Place
Santa Rosa, CA 95407
(800) 782-6748
www.psxdesign.com
ink pads, rubber stamps

QuickKutz
1454 West Business Park Drive
Orem, UT 84058
(888) 702-1146
www.quickkutz.com
die-cuts

Ranger Industries
15 Park Road
Tinton Falls, NJ 07724
(800) 244-2211
www.rangerink.com
ink pads, rubber stamps

Rebecca Sowers Fresh Cuts
EK Success
P.O. Box 1141
Clifton, NJ 07014-1141
www.eksuccess.com
printed paper embellishments

Rhode Island Textile
P.O. Box 999
Pawtucket, RI 02862-0999
(800) 556-6488
www.ritextile.com
hemp cord/twine

Rubber Stampede, Inc.
2550 Pellissier Place
Whittier, CA 90601
(800) 632-8386
www.rubberstampede.com
ink pads, rubber stamps

Sakura of America
30780 San Clemente Street
Hayward, CA 94544
(510) 475-8880
www.gellyroll.com
journaling and metallic pens

Sakura Japan
1-6-20, Morinomiya Chuo
Chuo-ku
Osaka, 540
81 (0) 6-6910-8824
www.craypas.com
journaling pens

SEI
1717 South 450 West
Logan, UT 84321
(800) 333-3279
www.shopsei.com
paper

Sizzix
c/o Ellison Craft & Design
25862 Commerce centre Drive
Lake Forest, CA 92630-8804
(866) 742-4447
www.sizzix.com
personal die-cutter and dies,
textured metallic paper

Stamper's Anonymous
Williamsburg Square
25967 Detroit Road
Westlake, OH 44145
(440) 250-9112
www.stampersanonymous.com
ink pads, rubber stamps

Stampin' Up
9350 South 150 East
Fifth Floor
Sandy, UT 84070
(801) 601-5353
www.stampinup.com
ink pads, rubber stamps

Sticklers
Scrapbook Times
1264 Tahoe Court
Orange Park, FL 32065
(904) 276-7990
www.scrapbooktimes.com
stickers

Strathmore Paper
(800) 808-3763
www.strathmore.com
paper

Two Peas in a Bucket, Inc.
2222 Evergreen Road
Suite 6
Middleton, WI 53562
(608) 827-0852
www.twopeasinabucket.com
computer fonts

Versamark by Tsukineko
Tsukineko, Inc.
17640 NE 65th Street
Redmond, WA 98052
(800) 769-6633 (U.S. and
Canada)
www.tsukineko.com
watermark ink pad

Tsukineko Co., Ltd.
(For orders outside North, South,
and Central America)
5-11-10 Arakawa, Arakawa-Ku
Tokyo 116, Japan
(03) 3891-4776
www.tsukineko.co.jp
ink pads, rubber stamps

Xyron
15820 North 84th Street
Scottsdale, AZ 85260
(800) 793-3523
www.xyron.com
adhesive machines

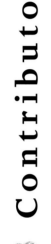

Contributors

Sandi Genovese
c/o Ellison Craft & Design
25862 Commercentre Drive
Lake Forest, CA 92630-8804
www.ellison.com
www.sizzix.com
(800) 253-2238

See author's biography on opposite page.

- - - - - - - - - - - - - - - - - - -

Andrea Grossman
Mrs. Grossman's Paper Company
3810 Cypress Drive
Petaluma, CA 94954
www.mrsgrossmans.com
(800) 457-4570

Andrea Grossman is the founder of Mrs. Grossman's Paper Company, the oldest sticker company in the United States, where she serves as president and art director.

- - - - - - - - - - - - - - - - - - -

Barb Wendel
Mrs. Grossman's Paper Company
3810 Cypress Drive
Petaluma, CA 94954
www.mrsgrossmans.com
(800) 457-4570

Barb Wendel is a sticker artist at Mrs. Grossman's Paper Company, where she has worked since 1999.

- - - - - - - - - - - - - - - - - - -

Becky Whaley-Butler
Independent Designer
27741 Sinsonte
Mission Viejo, CA 92692
(949) 457-8201

Becky Whaley-Butler is an avid scrapbooker who lives in Southern California. She worked in marketing for Ellison Craft & Design and her designs are currently featured on Sizzix.com.

- - - - - - - - - - - - - - - - - - -

Cara Mariano
c/o Ellison Craft & Design
25862 Commercentre Drive
Lake Forest, CA 92630-8804
www.ellison.com
www.sizzix.com
(800) 253-2238

Cara Mariano is an accomplished designer at Ellison Craft & Design with a degree in photography from California State University, Fullerton. Cara's designs have been featured in numerous Ellison and Sizzix ads and several popular magazines.

Carol Rice
Memory Technology, Inc.
32 E. Red Pine Drive
Alpine, UT 84004
www.memorybutton.com
(801) 756-6194

Carol Rice has been an innovator and award winner in the scrapbooking industry since 1991. She has had vast experience, first as an independent consultant and later as a co-owner of Memory Technology, Inc.

- - - - - - - - - - - - - - - - - - -

Dee Gruenig
Posh Impressions
22600-A Lambert Street
Suite 706
Lake Forest, CA 92630
www.poshimpressions.com
(949) 454-2609

A long-time craft industry expert, author, teacher, and television guest, Dee Gruenig has a Master of Arts degree from Stanford University. She is the owner of Posh Impressions and the designer of Posh Impressions Rubber Stamps.

- - - - - - - - - - - - - - - - - - -

Donna Downey
Scrapbooks by Design
13646 Toka Court
Huntersville, NC 28078
www.scrapbooksbydesign.com
(704) 947-7598

Donna Downey is a stay-at-home mom and runs a small scrapbooking-for-others company called Scrapbooks by Design to support her hobby.

- - - - - - - - - - - - - - - - - - -

E.L. Smith
c/o Ellison Craft & Design
25862 Commercentre Drive
Lake Forest, CA 92630-8804
www.ellison.com
www.sizzix.com
(800) 253-2238

E.L. Smith is the art director for Ellison Craft & Design and the accomplished illustrator of Ellison's full color project sheets. A graduate of Art Center School of Design in advertising, she is an avid watercolorist in her free time.

- - - - - - - - - - - - - - - - - - -

Grace Taormina
Rubber Stampede, Inc.
967-A Stanford Avenue
Oakland, CA 94608
www.rubberstampede.com
(800) 423-4135

Grace Taormina is the design director at Rubber Stampede, Inc. She is the author of *The Complete Guide to Rubber Stamping* and *The Complete Guide to Decorative Stamping.*

- - - - - - - - - - - - - - - - - - -

Jenna Beegle
c/o Anna Griffin, Inc.
733 Lambert Drive
Atlanta, GA 30324
www.annagriffin.com
(404) 817-8170

Jenna Beegle is a project designer for Anna Griffin, Inc., creating lovely things with beautiful papers. She teaches quilling, punch art, and heritage albums at her local scrapbook store and her work has been seen in Memory Makers, Somerset Studio, and several books.

- - - - - - - - - - - - - - - - - - -

Jennifer Mason
c/o Anna Griffin, Inc.
733 Lambert Drive
Atlanta, GA 30324
www.annagriffin.com
(404) 817-8170

Jennifer Mason, a project designer for Anna Griffin Inc., has a degree in graphic design, weaving, and textiles from the University of Michigan. Jennifer has been teaching paper art classes for five years, both in her own studio and at local stamp and scrapbook stores.

- - - - - - - - - - - - - - - - - - -

Julie Larsen
Making Memories
P.O. Box 1188
1168 West 500 North
Centerville, UT 84014
www.makingmemories.com
(801) 294-0430

Making Memories designers collaborated on these designs that incorporate the best of the company's popular Details collection. Making Memories, a 2001 Inc. 500 winner, is one of the nation's fastest-growing scrapbook and craft supply manufacturers.

- - - - - - - - - - - - - - - - - - -

Kelly Carolla
Mrs. Grossman's Paper Company
3810 Cypress Drive
Petaluma, CA 94954
www.mrsgrossmans.com
(800) 457-4570

Kelly Carolla is a sticker artist at Mrs. Grossman's Paper Company, where she has worked since 2001. Kelly has a strong background in product development and merchandising, in addition to extensive experience in crafts and stamping.

- - - - - - - - - - - - - - - - - -

Kelly Jones
basj1995@yahoo.com

Kelly Jones calls herself a true scrapaholic. She has been published in *Ivy Cottage Creations*, *Creating Keepsakes*, and is a regular contributor in *Scrapbooks ETC*.

- - - - - - - - - - - - - - - - - -

Michele Gerbrandt
Memory Makers magazine
and books
12365 N. Huron Street, #500
Denver, CO 80234
www.memorymakersmagazine.com
(303) 452-1968

In 1995, Michele Gerbrandt recognized that the national scrapbooking community would benefit from an idea resource magazine—thus the first scrapbook magazine, *Memory Makers*, was born. Michele co-hosts the *Scrapbook Memories* TV series for PBS and is a regular guest on HGTV's *The Carol Duvall Show* and DIY's *Scrapbooking*.

- - - - - - - - - - - - - - - - - -

Shelli Gardner
www.stampinup.com

Shelli Gardner is the CEO and cofounder for Stampin' Up!, one of the nation's leading manufacturers and distributors of decorative rubber stamps.

- - - - - - - - - - - - - - - - - -

Sherryl Kumli
c/o Mrs. Grossman's Paper
Company
3810 Cypress Drive
Petaluma, CA 94954
www.mrsgrossmans.com
(800) 457-4570

Sherryl Kumli is the coordinator of the sticker art department and assistant to Andrea Grossman at Mrs. Grossman's Paper Company, where she has worked since 1999.

- - - - - - - - - - - - - - - - - -

Stephanie Barnard
Stephanie's Scraps
28461 El Peppino
Laguna Niguel, CA 92677
skbarn@juno.com
(949) 831-2230

Stephanie Barnard is an accomplished author, designer, and teacher. She has written a book published by Design Originals, as well as co-authoring many other books. Her work appears in several top industry magazines.

PHOTO BY JACK PARKER; COURTESY OF DIY–DO IT YOURSELF NETWORK

About the author

Sandi Genovese is a multitalented artist, author, and educator. She is the senior vice president and creative director of Ellison Craft & Design and hosts the daily television series *Scrapbooking* on the Do-It-Yourself (DIY) Network. She has written several books, including *Simply Sizzix*, *Creative Scrapbooking*, *Memories in Minutes*, and *Creative Greeting Cards*, and is a frequent contributor to scrapbook magazines. Sandi often appears as a guest on HGTV's *The Carol Duvall Show* and has demonstrated scrapbooking techniques on ABC's *Good Morning America*, *The View*, and other popular programs. She received Creating Keepsakes Magazine's 2001 Outstanding Achievement Award for her lifelong contributions to scrapbooking and is a passionate ambassador for the craft.

Acknowledgments

Thank you to each of the artists whose unique creations give life to the pages of this book. I'm awed by their creativity and their eagerness to share their time and their work.

A special thank you to Laurie Weathersby. Not only is she a delight to work with, but her assistance with all the details and her organizational skills were invaluable to me in connecting the diverse styles in the projects in this book.

I'd also like to thank Heather Reeves Hawkins, whose writing inspires me and who helped me to sort out what I really wanted to say.

In addition, I'd like to thank Mary Ann Hall at Rockport Publishers, who patiently worked around my crazy schedule and guided me through the paperwork necessary to complete this book.

And of course, thanks to Lindsay Stoms, my copyeditor, whose attention to detail is amazing.

I'd also like to thank LaDorna and Bob Eichenberg and Lisa Corcoran at Ellison for giving me a creative home and the freedom to work on this book.

Finally, I'd like to thank my parents, Jess and Connie Fuhriman, for their love and the greatest gift of all—the belief that anything in life is possible.